SAM HOLCROFT

Sam Holcroft's other plays include *Rules for Living* at the National Theatre; *The Wardrobe*, part of the National Theatre Connections Festival; *Edgar & Annabel*, part of the *Double Feature* season in the Paintframe at the National Theatre; *Dancing Bears*, part of the *Charged* season for Clean Break at Soho Theatre and Latitude Festival; *While You Lie* at the Traverse, Edinburgh; *Pink*, part of the *Women, Power and Politics* season at the Tricycle; *Vanya*, adapted from Chekhov, at the Gate; and *Cockroach*, co-produced by the National Theatre of Scotland and the Traverse (nominated for Best New Play 2008, by the Critics' Awards for Theatre in Scotland and shortlisted for the John Whiting Award, 2009). In 2013, Sam wrote *The House Taken Over*, a libretto for opera, adapted from Cortázar, for the Festival d'Aix-en-Provence and Académie Européenne de Musique. Sam received the Tom Erhardt Award in 2009, was the Pearson Writer-in-Residence at the Traverse Theatre from 2009–10, and the Writer-in-Residence at the National Theatre Studio from 2013–14. In 2014, Sam received a Windham Campbell Prize for Literature in the drama category.

Sam Holcroft

A MIRROR

NICK HERN BOOKS

London

www.nickhernbooks.co.uk

A Nick Hern Book

A Mirror first published as a paperback original in Great Britain in 2023 by Nick Hern Books Limited, The Glasshouse, 49a Goldhawk Road, London W12 8QP

A Mirror © 2023 Sam Holcroft

Sam Holcroft has asserted her right to be identified as the author of this work

Cover: Jonny Lee Miller photographed by Sebastian Nevols. Concept by Émilie Chen.

Designed and typeset by Nick Hern Books, London
Printed in Great Britain by Mimeo Ltd, Huntingdon, Cambridgeshire PE29 6XX

A CIP catalogue record for this book is available from the British Library

ISBN   978 1 83904 266 9

www.nickhernbooks.co.uk/environmental-policy

A Mirror was first performed at the Almeida Theatre, London, on 15 August 2023, with the following cast:

WEDDING GUEST	Sara Houghton
ČELIK	Jonny Lee Miller
SENIOR OFFICER	Aaron Neil
MEI	Tanya Reynolds
BAX	Geoffrey Streatfeild
MUSICIAN	Miriam Wakeling
ADEM	Micheal Ward
With	Sarah Carvalho
	Aimee Dore
	Mariella Dyckhoff
	Evans Nwogu
	Zak Shetewi
	Elliot Tamatave
	Kyle Walsh

Director	Jeremy Herrin
Set and Costume Designer	Max Jones
Lighting Designer	Azusa Ono
Composer and Sound Designer	Nick Powell
Fight Director	Jonathan Holby
Casting Director	Jessica Ronane
Costume Supervisor	Cáit Canavan
Assistant Director	Molly Stacey
Associate Designer	Ruth Hall
Casting Associate	Abby Galvin
Casting Assistants	Poppy Apter and Mary Clapp

Acknowledgements

I first visited Lebanon in April 2014, at the invitation of Elyse Dodgson, the indomitable International Director of the Royal Court Theatre. Elyse had arranged a week-long writing workshop, led by her frequent collaborator, David Greig, for a hand-picked group of Lebanese and Syrian writers.

The role of 'the Ministry' loomed large in our discussions with these writers. Both Syria and Lebanon operate systems of state censorship. Writers must submit their scripts to a censorship bureau within the Ministry of Culture for approval.

One playwright and film-maker attending our workshop, Lucien Bourjeily, had grown so frustrated with Lebanon's censors that he wrote a satire set *inside* the censorship bureau – called *Will It Pass Or Not?* And then, in a truly heroic display of cheek, submitted that play to the Ministry for approval. It was (naturally) banned immediately. And Lucien's passport was subsequently confiscated.

A Mirror is partly inspired by Lucien's act of bravery, and I'd like to thank him for giving this project his blessing. His courage, and that of thousands of artists like him, around the world, both inspires and intimidates me – because I suspect, deep down, that I do not possess it. I'd also like to emphasise that the character of Adem is not Lucien, that *A Mirror* is not set in Lebanon, and that the events depicted in the play are entirely fictional.

I'd like to acknowledge the influence of Yuval Noah Harari's book *Sapiens* on Mr Čelik's views regarding the power of storytelling. Mr Čelik's speeches on pages 43–44, in particular, owe a great deal to Mr Harari's ideas.

Thanks to Martin Bright and Lumli Lumlong for illuminating conversations about the censorship of art and journalism. I'd like to thank the (many) people who've helped me shape the text of this play: Mel Kenyon, Zephy Losey, Jeremy Herrin, Rupert Goold, Stephanie Bain and Vicky Featherstone.

Finally, I'd like to thank my husband, Alastair Blyth. As Adem says to Čelik, 'So many of the words were yours, I couldn't claim all the credit.' But I have, and you let me. Thank you.

S.H.

For Lucien Bourjeily
A braver writer than I will ever be

And for Elyse Dodgson
Who inspired playwrights around the world
(Including this one)

Characters

ČELIK/REGISTRAR, *male*
ADEM/GROOM, *male*
MEI/BRIDE, *female*
BAX/BEST MAN, *male*
SENIOR OFFICER, *male*
WEDDING GUEST
MUSICIAN
OFFICER PETROV *and* AGENTS OF THE COMMISSION
    FOR PUBLIC ORDER (CPO)

A forward slash (/) marks the point of interruption in
overlapping dialogue.

*This text went to press before the end of rehearsals and so may
differ slightly from the play as performed.*

Prelude

A wedding venue, plain and modestly decorated. Rows of seating either side of an aisle, leading up to a raised platform. A desk and three chairs arranged on the platform, adorned with flowers and candles. A MUSICIAN *plays gentle music.*

The audience are greeted as if they are guests at a wedding service – (bride or groom?) From now on, the audience will be referred to as the WEDDING GUESTS. *They are shown to their seats by members of the* WEDDING PARTY *and provided with service sheets titled 'The Wedding of Leyla and Joel'.*

The REGISTRAR *wanders the stage. He is a distinguished-looking man, wearing a slightly worn three-piece suit and leather gloves. Alongside him is a younger man, the* GROOM, *in a cheap, poorly fitting suit. They nod and smile (a little nervously) at various* GUESTS.

When the last of the GUESTS *has arrived, the* REGISTRAR *is given a signal by the* BEST MAN *(who is a little older than the* GROOM). *The music stops and the* REGISTRAR *steps forward to address the* WEDDING GUESTS.

REGISTRAR. Would you all please stand for the Entrance of the Bride.

The WEDDING GUESTS *stand. The* MUSICIAN *plays entrance music, as the rear doors open, and the* BRIDE *steps into the room. She wears a modest white dress, clutches a simple bouquet. Smiles nervously at the* GUESTS *as she steps down the aisle.*

The GROOM *smiles lovingly as she reaches his side – and they turn to face the* REGISTRAR. *The* MUSICIAN *concludes the song and the* REGISTRAR *addresses the* GUESTS.

Would you all please be seated.

The WEDDING GUESTS *sit.*

Ladies and gentlemen, friends and family, welcome to you all. And thank you for coming today to share this wonderful occasion. We are here to witness and celebrate the union of this man and this woman, in this venue which has been duly sanctioned for the celebration of marriage. If any person present knows of any reason why they should not be married according to the law, then they should declare it now.

The WEDDING GUESTS *remain silent.*

Leyla and Joel, before you are joined in matrimony, I must remind you both of the solemn and binding character of the vows you are about to make. Marriage, in this country, means the union of two people, voluntarily entered into for life. I am now going to ask each of you in turn to declare that you know of no legal reason why you may not be joined together in marriage. (*To the* GROOM.) Joel, please repeat after me: I do solemnly declare…

GROOM. I do solemnly declare…

REGISTRAR. Of my own accord and without coercion…

GROOM. Of my own accord and without coercion…

REGISTRAR. According to the constitution of this country…

GROOM. According to the constitution of this country…

REGISTRAR. And the oath I have sworn to its people, and its leadership…

GROOM. And the oath I have sworn to its people, and its leadership…

REGISTRAR. That I know not of any lawful impediment…

GROOM. That I know not of any lawful impediment…

REGISTRAR. Why I Joel…

GROOM. Why I Joel…

REGISTRAR. May not be joined in marriage to Leyla.

GROOM. May not be joined in marriage to Leyla.

REGISTRAR. Thank you, Joel. (*To the* BRIDE.) Leyla, please repeat after me. I do solemnly declare…

BRIDE. I do solemnly d–…

A GUEST *stands. The* BRIDE *looks his way, distracted for a moment – but the* GUEST *doesn't even glance at her, or make any apology for the interruption. After a moment of silence, the* REGISTRAR *nods towards the standing* GUEST.

REGISTRAR. Officer.

GUEST (*waving his hand dismissively, heading for the exit*). Carry on.

REGISTRAR (*to the* BRIDE). I do solemnly declare…

BRIDE. I do solemnly declare…

REGISTRAR. Of my own accord and without coercion…

BRIDE. Of my own accord and without coercion…

The GUEST *exits, the door swinging loudly shut behind him.*

REGISTRAR. According to the constitution of this country…

BRIDE. According to constitution of this country…

The GROOM *and* REGISTRAR *look towards the* BEST MAN *– who skirts the edge of the room to the rear doors, and pokes his head outside.*

REGISTRAR. And the oath I have sworn to its people, and its leadership…

BRIDE. And the oath I have sworn to its people, and its leadership…

REGISTRAR. That I know not of any lawful impediment…

BRIDE. That I know not of any lawful impediment…

The BEST MAN *gives a thumbs-up to the* GROOM *and* REGISTRAR, *and closes the rear doors. The* REGISTRAR, GROOM *and* BRIDE *quickly leave the stage, removing the flowers and candles from the table as they do so. The* BEST MAN *addresses the* WEDDING GUESTS –

BEST MAN. Thank you, everyone, for your patience – we'll be starting in a few moments.

To the side of the stage, the REGISTRAR, GROOM *and* BRIDE *are swiftly helping each other change costume. The* GROOM *removes his tie and jacket, leaving only a plain shirt and trousers. The* BRIDE *helps the* REGISTRAR *to adorn his blazer with insignia.*

Before we do, let me say how much we appreciate your presence here tonight. We know the risk that each and every one of you is taking, and we salute your courage. This performance is being staged without a licence from the Ministry. Anyone previously unaware of this should please feel free to leave now.

The WEDDING GUESTS *are given the opportunity to leave – anyone who wants to can.*

The BRIDE *pulls a simple blazer over her dress, her wedding outfit now looking more like office attire. The* BRIDE *and* GROOM *slide the table centre-stage, placing chairs either side.*

Without further ado, we present to you – '*A Play*'.

There may be some muted applause from the audience as the BRIDE, GROOM *and* BEST MAN *leave the stage. The* BEST MAN *dims the lights from the back of the room – but angled lights remain focused on the platform/stage.*

The play begins.

Scene One

Mr Čelik's office, Ministry of Culture. A few desk accessories, including an intercom device, an engraved name plate and vase of flowers, all suggest this is the office of a senior-ranking official.

MEI (*played by the* BRIDE) *enters. She has a stiff, military bearing. She's closely followed by* ADEM (*played by the* GROOM), *who appears nervous.*

MEI. You can wait in here – Mr Čelik will join you shortly.

ADEM. Right. (*Beat.*) Sorry – who?

MEI. The Director. Mr Čelik.

ADEM. The… sorry, the director of… plays?

MEI. Of the Ministry.

    ADEM *looks alarmed.*

ADEM. The *Ministry*?

MEI. Yes. He won't be long. His meeting with the Minister started late.

ADEM. Sorry, excuse me, is that… is this normal?

MEI. Yes, I think the Minister often runs late.

ADEM. No, I mean is it normal for someone like me to meet with the Director of the Ministry? Am I… Have I done something wrong?

MEI. I wouldn't know.

ADEM. Please, anything you can tell me would –

MEI. This is my second week here, I don't even work on this floor… I don't know what's standard procedure.

ADEM. But if I *had* done something wrong, then would this be the sort of thing which… No, okay. Sorry. I shouldn't have asked.

    A beat, then MEI *exits.*

ADEM *looks around anxiously. He goes to sit down – but can't decide on which chair. He chooses one… changes his mind… chooses another. He smooths his shirt, and waits.*

ČELIK *enters* (*played by the* REGISTRAR, *still wearing his three-piece suit and leather gloves*). ADEM *immediately stands, bowing his head in deference.* MEI *enters behind* ČELIK, *carrying several folders and papers, which she lays on the desk, turning to the appropriate pages.*

ČELIK. Mr Nariman. Hello, my name is Mr Čelik.

ADEM. Pleased to meet you, sir.

ČELIK *heads straight for his desk, without shaking hands.* ADEM *stands ramrod straight.*

ČELIK. Please sit – we don't stand to attention here, this is the Ministry for *Culture* not the Ministry of Defence. (*To* MEI.) Thank you, Mei, I think that's all we need – for now. Wait outside please.

MEI *nods briskly and exits.* ADEM *sits.*

Now, Mr Nariman – may I call you Adem?

ADEM. Yes, sir. Of course.

ČELIK. None of this 'Yes sir, no sir', 'Mr Čelik' is fine. Now, Adem, I expect you know why you're here?

ADEM. I, um… not… completely.

ČELIK. But you are Mr Adem Nariman? You did write a play titled *The Ninth Floor* and submit it to the Ministry two months ago? This isn't a case of mistaken identity?

ADEM. Oh, no – I mean, yes. That's me. I did that. Because I thought… I mean, I was told that's… what you're supposed to do. When you write a play. Is that… Did I do something wrong?

A pause as ČELIK *scrutinises* ADEM *from across the desk.* ADEM *fidgets nervously.*

ČELIK. Usually, at this stage in the process, you'd receive a letter from the Ministry, perhaps inviting you to meet with

one of our junior Readers. But in your case, the Reader in
question felt it necessary to pass your script to her
Supervisor, who passed it up to his Section Head, and from
there it flew up every rung on the ladder, until it landed on
my desk.

ADEM (*quietly horrified*). R… right.

ČELIK *continues to scrutinise* ADEM.

(*Swallowing back unease.*) I'm sorry, sir, Mr Čelik… Am
I in some kind of trouble?

ČELIK *searches* ADEM*'s face for something – but doesn't
seem to find an answer. He looks down at the papers in front
of him.*

ČELIK. It says here that you're… a mechanic by trade – is that
correct?

ADEM. That's right.

ČELIK. Cars? Or agricultural equipment?

ADEM. Oh, er… cars mostly. Some bikes. Once a tank, but
only because it broke down outside the garage.

ČELIK *smiles.*

ČELIK (*checking his papers*). But you used to be in the army?

ADEM (*unnerved*). Um… yes, Engineer Corps. Specialist,
Four-Six Battalion. But I completed my service two years
ago. I'm a plain old mechanic now. More carburettors, fewer
landmines.

ADEM *attempts a laugh,* ČELIK *watches him.*

ČELIK. Actually, I have a problem with my car.

ADEM (*suddenly hopeful*). Really?

ČELIK. It's making a knocking noise under the pedals. For
about two weeks.

ADEM. Is that why I'm here – to fix your car?

ČELIK. No, no, it's just – while you're here.

ADEM. Oh. Well… sounds like your suspension bolt's about to shear. You should get that looked at.

ČELIK. The Ministry's repair plant says it's nothing to worry about.

ADEM (*hastily*). Well, I'm sure they know what they're talking about, of course. But I'd get it looked at all the same. Unscrewing a weak bolt takes thirty seconds, but once it shears you'll have to drill it, punch it, and rethread it – could take hours. Weeks if the part's unavailable. But you can repurpose one from another model if you know what you're doing.

ČELIK. You can tell all of that just from a knocking sound?

ADEM. Well, it's a common problem these days with the roads being… the way they are. And with replacement parts hard to come by, what with the shortages… it's better to fix it before it fails. I see it as part of the service: it's my job to know the breaking point of things.

A short pause.

ČELIK. But when you're not repairing cars – or tanks – you also harbour literary aspirations.

ADEM. I don't know about that.

ČELIK. Is this the first play you've written? It's the first you've submitted to the Ministry – but is there a stack of Nariman manuscripts in a desk drawer somewhere?

ADEM. No, this is… it's the first one.

ČELIK *considers this.*

ČELIK. A combat engineer, turned mechanic, turned playwright… Explain that to me. (*Off* ADEM*'s confusion.*) What was it that made you put down your spanners and pick up a pen, to write a piece of theatre?

ADEM. I… don't know.

ČELIK. Have you always enjoyed the arts? Do you go to the theatre often?

ADEM *shifts uncomfortably in his seat, somewhat embarrassed.*

ADEM. Um... no, not... I'm – To be honest, I haven't seen much theatre. Sorry. I'm more of a film person. But the equipment is expensive. The camera alone costs, well, more than I can afford, and then there's the lenses, tripods, microphones. But a play – all you need is a stage, right? I figured if I wrote a play it might actually get made. Sorry, that's probably not what you wanted to hear.

ČELIK *weighs his response.*

ČELIK. Film, television, theatre – the Ministry welcomes all forms of storytelling. (*Beat.*) So let's take a look at it, shall we? (*Reading from the script.*) *The Ninth Floor* by Adem Nariman. Intriguing title – *The Ninth Floor.* Perhaps you could talk a little bit about what made you choose this particular milieu for your first dramatic work?

ADEM. Um. 'Mill-yoo'...?

ČELIK. The place, the people – why did you write about these people, and this particular place, rather than anywhere else?

ADEM. Oh, well, that's easy – they're people I know. I mean, it's sort of about my building. The people who live where I live. Is that not... how you're supposed to do it?

Beat.

ČEILK. Let's read a bit, shall we? (*Pressing the intercom button.*) Mei, could you come in here, please? (*Releasing the intercom button.*) It's always useful for a writer to hear their work out loud.

MEI *enters.*

Mei, we could use your assistance. Would you mind reading a section of Adem's play with us?

MEI (*alarmed*). Read...? Out loud?

ČELIK. Yes, that's right. (*Handing* MEI *pages of script.*) And pass these around, please.

MEI. But I'm not an actor, sir.

ČELIK. I know that.

MEI. I… I don't act.

ČELIK. You don't need to act, Mei, you just need to read aloud.

MEI. I'm not – I don't do / that either –

ČELIK. Let's turn to page twenty-one, Scene Four, and we'll read from the top.

MEI *looks somewhat distraught as she offers* ADEM *a script, before selecting the correct page for* ČELIK, *and then for herself. She sits.*

Adem, why don't you read the character 'Soldier'. Mei, could you please read the character 'Prostitute'. And I'll read the stage directions. Alright. (*Clearing his throat, reading stage directions from the script.*) Scene Four. A cramped studio apartment on the ninth floor of a high-rise block in the North District. Against one wall is a worn kitchen counter with a two-ring hob and a small sink, encrusted with limescale. The tap is held upright by black tape. The green carpet is darkened by spreading watermarks from the leaking radiator, the white ceiling mottled with black mould. In one corner, two naked bodies writhe awkwardly on a sofa – a young man, rough around the edges, and a skinny woman, aged before her time. As she rides him, close to completion, he suddenly cries out, not with ecstasy, but in pain.

Pause.

Mei? It's your line.

MEI. Yes, sir. Sorry, sir. (*Clearing her throat, reading.*) Prostitute. Stopping mid-thrust –

ČELIK (*interrupting*). Mei, you needn't read the character name or any stage directions in brackets. If the stage directions are relevant, I'll read them.

MEI. So I just…?

ČELIK. You just read the dialogue.

MEI. The dialogue. Thank you, sir.

MEI *is a poor sight-reader, her performance is stilted, stumbling, sometimes mispronouncing words.*

(*Reading as Prostitute.*) What… what's wrong? Are you okay?

ADEM (*reading as Soldier*). Fuck, stop, stop! Please, just…

MEI (*reading*). What's the matter?

ADEM (*reading*). Just get the fuck off me. Now.

ČELIK (*reading*). The Prostitute clambers off the Soldier. He curls into a ball, gasping for breath, clutching his leg, which is streaked with scars.

MEI (*reading*). Shit, are you alright? Do you want me to – ?

ADEM (*reading*). Don't touch me. I said don't fucking touch me, can't you see I'm in fucking agony?

MEI. (*reading*). Alright. Alright. (*Looking up at* ČELIK.) It says 'Pause'.

ČELIK. You can just take a pause.

MEI *nods and they take a long pause.* MEI *seems unsure how long one should last.*

That will be sufficient, thank you, Mei.

MEI (*nods, continues reading*). Look, are you gonna be alright or what?

ADEM (*reading*). It'll pass in a minute. It's the shrapnel – I told you not to put your weight on my thigh.

MEI (*reading*). Sorry, I didn't realise that was why.

ADEM (*reading*). I'm due another surgery, but the waiting list's as long as a fucking cunt.

MEI (*reading*). You bring any painkillers?

ADEM (*reading*). The Vets' Clinic gave me fucking baby aspirin. 'Emergencies only.' I doubt whore-induced cramping counts as an emergency. (*Beat*.) Sorry. I didn't mean to call you… It just. Hurts.

MEI (*reading*). I have some pills. My mum had a full prescription when she died. Bone cancer, so they're pretty full-on. Sort you out in fifteen minutes. Then we could finish.

ADEM (*reading*). Yes, yes, give me one. I wanna finish.

MEI (*reading*). Give? I'm not a charity. You want pills, you pay for them.

ADEM (*reading*). Come on, do me a favour.

MEI (*reading*). Favours don't put food in my daughter's mouth.

ADEM (*reading*). Half a pill then?

MEI (*reading*). I'm not doing that.

ADEM (*reading*). Have you got a screwdriver?

MEI (*reading*). I said I'm not crushing it up all over the place.

ADEM (*reading*). I'll fix your radiator. Or do you want to wait for building maintenance, and fucking freeze?

MEI (*reading*). Fine, do that first, then I'll give you a pill.

ADEM (*reading*). I need the pill first if I'm gonna be lifting a radiator off the wall.

MEI (*reading*). Here, take it. If you fix the radiator you can fuck me.

ČELIK. I think that's a good place to stop. Thank you, Mei.

MEI *nods and stands immediately to leave*.

(*To* MEI.) Don't leave, Mei, it would be useful to hear your reaction.

MEI. *My* reaction?

ČELIK. Yes.

MEI *sits, dismayed*.

How did that make you feel, Mei?

MEI. Um. I… I don't know.

ČELIK. There's no right or wrong answer. Just your initial reaction. How did it feel to read that?

MEI. Um… uncomfortable.

ČELIK. Uncomfortable. Thank you, Mei. Was that the intended effect, Adem?

ADEM. Sorry?

ČELIK. Is that how you wanted your audience to feel – uncomfortable?

ADEM. Er. No, not really.

ČELIK. Then what did you want them to feel?

ADEM. I'm… not really sure.

ČELIK. I'm trying to get at your intention, Adem. What was your *intention* in writing this scene?

ADEM. I didn't really have one.

ČELIK. Of course you did, you wrote it. You chose these particular characters, in this particular place, saying and doing these particular things – why?

ADEM. It's just… what they did.

ČELIK. What who did?

ADEM. My neighbours.

ČELIK. So… hang on, this is based on a real event, is it?

ADEM. It is the real event.

ČELIK. Are you the soldier? Did this happen to you?

ADEM. No, not to me, no, to my neighbour. I heard it through the wall. I live in one of the old Union Buildings, the walls are paper-thin, you can hear everything that goes on either side of you.

ČELIK (*finally understanding*). So you didn't make this up? These are things people actually said, conversations you've overheard, word-for-word?

ADEM. Yeah, yes.

ČELIK. Does that go for all these scenes? The deranged man who never goes outside? The widow who feeds the stray dogs?

ADEM. Yeah, they're my neighbours. Him on one side; the old lady is below; and on the other side, the woman in the scene we read. She's a hairdresser during the day, but sometimes she brings clients home. I hear them talking through the wall and I just wrote down what I heard.

Beat. ČELIK *watches* ADEM *closely.*

ČELIK. Okay, I'm beginning to understand, you eavesdrop on your neighbours through / the wall –

ADEM. Not by choice, you just... can't help hearing everything everyone does.

ČELIK. So you *hear* your neighbours through the wall, and you 'just' write down what you hear...

ADEM. I'm sorry, I shouldn't have... I don't want to get anyone in trouble.

ČELIK. I'm not asking about the conduct of your neighbours, Adem, I'm asking about you, *your* dramatic choices. Why include *these* moments, *these* conversations in your play, when presumably you've overheard hundreds. Clearly you've been selective, my question is: for what effect?

ADEM. Er. I... I guess they were the ones that stuck out in my memory.

ČELIK. Stuck out why?

ADEM. I don't know. I just kept thinking about them.

ČELIK. I'm not surprised. Each of these conversations is shocking in its own way. In the course of just sixty pages we have... (*Flicking through the script.*) prostitution, drug dealing, gambling, child neglect, an attempted suicide and a compulsive masturbator perforating his bowel with a chair leg up his rectum. Tell me, Adem, do you hate your neighbourhood?

ADEM. What? No. I love my neighbourhood.

ČELIK. Then why do you write about it this way?

ADEM. Because it *is* this way.

A pause as ČELIK *scrutinises* ADEM *over the rim of his glasses.*

ČELIK. And whom do you blame for that?

ADEM. Blame?

ČELIK. The Veterans' Clinic? The Ministry of Housing? Whose fault is it? Do you want the audience to be angry with someone in particular?

ADEM. No.

ČELIK. Are *you* angry with someone in particular?

ADEM. No.

ČELIK. Do you hate your country, Adem?

ADEM. Do I – What? No. No, I don't hate my country, I love my country. I fought for it. My grandfather, my father, we've all served. I honestly just… my *intention* was just… to make something real. And, and, to me, what I heard through the wall was… real.

ČELIK *holds* ADEM*'s gaze for a long time, before coming to a decision.*

ČELIK. Alright.

ČELIK*'s demeanour changes – he seems to relax, soften.*

Look, ordinarily, you'd have received a rejection letter from the Ministry. And quite possibly a visit from the CPO.

ČELIK *nods to* MEI *who serves* ADEM *with a letter.* ADEM *opens it, skim-reads –*

ADEM (*reading aloud from the letter*). '…Please be advised that the Committee has read your play script and observed that it is indecent, offensive and calculated to undermine the peace and security of the State. Please report immediately to the Commission for Public Order.'

ADEM *lowers the letter, a look of bewilderment on his face.*

'Calculated to undermine the peace and security of the State'…?

ČELIK. I can just about believe – *just* – that you're naive enough not to realise this play is completely unstageable.

ADEM. Oh.

ČELIK. Firstly, and frankly most trivially, because this script is so profane it would contravene both the Theatres Act and Article Twelve of the Penal Code. Mei can give you the booklet on proscribed speech. Tedious, I know, but rules are rules.

MEI *hands* ADEM *a booklet.*

ADEM. But… people curse. That's how they speak.

ČELIK. Maybe. But you're talking about surface truth, mere verisimilitude.

ADEM. I'm afraid I… don't think I understand.

ČELIK. Let's imagine your play was performed at a public theatre – the main stage of Unity Hall. Twelve hundred seats, full to capacity every night, for sixteen weeks. That's one hundred and thirty thousand people. They arrive in the auditorium with their worries and cares rattling around in their heads. What are they there for? To be reminded of the petty imperfections of their everyday lives? Or – to be transported, moved, entertained – and in the end, *elevated.* Inspired to look at their own lives in a new light.

ADEM. It sounds like… you think it's the second one.

ČELIK. If they wanted 'reality' they could sit on their own stairwells and listen to their neighbours. They came to a theatre to experience something deeper. Art doesn't merely tell you what *is*, but what *could be*. And that, I'm afraid, is the fundamental problem with your play. Profanities aside, on a purely artistic level, your play – to put it as gently as possible – fails completely.

ADEM. Oh. Right. (*Then.*) Can you… be more specific?

ČELIK. I could. But it would be a waste of both our time. Lack of structure, lack of story, characters without arcs, no tension, no resolution. But the writing itself / is actually –

ADEM. Please don't. I get it: it's awful.

ČELIK. No. It's actually quite good.

ADEM. What?

ČELIK. A little raw but, for a first attempt, fairly impressive. You show a certain flair for atmosphere – the settings and character descriptions are concise, but evocative. To speak in your language, Adem: you have the tools, you just need to put them to the proper use, on the right vehicle.

ADEM. So… are you saying I should write it again?

ČELIK. No, definitely not. This play is what you'd call 'a write-off'. But I know how crushing a rejection letter can be. And I *hate* to see promising writers get discouraged. So I wanted to see you in person to make it crystal clear that while your play is being rejected, *you* are not.

ADEM.…Thank you.

ČELIK. This Ministry exists to nurture new talent, not extinguish it. I'm in the process of securing funds for a new development programme – to offer mentoring, workshops, rehearsal space and actors to promising writers. We've done this on an informal basis before, with writers who've gone on to become national treasures: Garcia, Pejman, Bax –

ADEM*'s head snaps up at this.*

You've heard of Bax?

ADEM. Of course. We studied one of his plays at school: *The Market Trader of Unity Square*.

ČELIK. Aha, his first great success. And mine, as it happens. Back when I worked on the second floor, as Mei does now, it was one of the first plays to cross my desk.

ADEM. I think it's beautiful.

ČELIK. I agree. But notice the word you just used – 'beautiful'.
The story of a humble carpenter, peddling trinkets from
a shabby stall in the gutter – the kind of man you might pass
a hundred times and never notice. Bax takes that little man's
beleaguered life, sifts through the filth, the poverty and pain
like a miner panning through slurry, and unearths – gems.
Tiny acts of courage and kindness. Shows us all that a man is
defined, not by his station in life, but by his actions. And that
any one of us can be a hero. If that isn't an inspiration to us
all, I don't know what is.

ČELIK *stands*. ADEM *automatically does the same*.

I'm afraid our time's up, but please – send me something new.
Send it directly to me, I'll read it personally. Just a scene, or
a fragment, a couple of pages would be fine – but make it
something hopeful, something inspiring. (*Indicating* ADEM*'s
script*.) You've shown me the filth. Now show me the beauty.
Give me just one speck of noble grit – and I'll help you craft
a pearl.

ADEM. Thank you, sir, Director Čelik. I'll try to do that.

ČELIK. Make sure you do. Good to meet you, Adem.

ADEM *exits*. MEI *collects the papers from the desk*.

MEI. If that's all, sir?

MEI *heads for the exit*.

ČELIK. Actually, Mei, stay a moment please.

MEI. Certainly, sir.

MEI *stands stiffly to attention*.

ČELIK. Tell me, how did you find that?

MEI. Find what, sir?

ČELIK. The meeting – what did you think?

MEI (*cautious*). I… thought it was… good, sir.

ČELIK. I'm not looking for vague compliments, Mei – the Ministry has lickspittles to spare. You can be honest. In fact, I insist on it.

MEI. Honestly, sir, I found it… surprising.

ČELIK. Better. Surprising, how?

MEI. Well, to be candid, sir, I thought he was in trouble. When I first read his script, I flagged one hundred and twelve infractions – Forbidden Language, Hostile Material and Politically Sensitive Content. So when I handed the script to my supervisor, Mr Garmash –

ČELIK. Ah yes, the inimitable Mr Garmash.

MEI. – when I passed the script up to him, according to protocol, he found a further twenty-nine. He recommends Mr Nariman be arrested immediately, questioned by the Commission for Public Order, and assigned to a re-education facility.

ČELIK. Do you think I mishandled it, then?

MEI. Oh no, sir, no… the opposite.

   ČELIK *smiles at this*.

ČELIK. How long have you been assigned here?

MEI. Two weeks, sir.

ČELIK. And before that you were…?

MEI. I was a Field Armourer, Private First Class. Forward Base Delta.

ČELIK (*surprised*). On the border?

MEI. Yes, sir.

ČELIK. You fought on the front lines and they reassigned you to the Ministry of *Culture*?

MEI. Medical discharge, sir. Repeat stress fractures in my right leg and knee – I can't train any more, sir.

ČELIK. You needn't call me 'sir'. 'Mr Čelik' will do just fine.

MEI. Yes, sir. Mr Čelik.

ČELIK. How do you feel about your new assignment? I take it you had no say in the matter?

MEI. No, Mr Čelik, but I'm grateful. Whatever my country needs of me.

ČELIK. Still, it must be quite the change, getting issued with a packet of highlighters instead of a crate of rifles?

MEI. Less than you'd think, Mr Čelik. In the Corps I was given a checklist for stripping and cleaning rifles; when I arrived at the Censor Bureau, I was given a checklist for reviewing plays.

ČELIK *winces at the words 'Censor Bureau'.*

ČELIK. I know that's what the public calls us – 'the Censor Bureau'…

MEI. Sorry, sir, is that not – ?

ČELIK. No, no, it's not your fault. It's the fault of people like Mr Garmash – who think plays can be appraised with a checklist. It's this relentless fixation on the negative – what we *can't* say, what we *mustn't* show – that I've been struggling to change. We're not 'the Censor Bureau', we're the Ministry of Culture. I believe we can do a lot more to live up to that title. (*Beat. Off* MEI*'s slightly bewildered expression.*) Do you like theatre, Mei? Have you ever been?

MEI. Um. Yes, once. Or, I mean… the theatre came to me. To my unit. The AF… C-something? I can't remember the name –

ČELIK. Armed Forces Entertainment Corps.

MEI. Yeah, they had a band and a comedian and a little play at the end.

ČELIK. What did you think of it?

MEI. It was good.

ČELIK. I asked you to be honest. I'm not trying to trap you.

MEI. It was… a bit… annoying, I guess?

ČELIK. Annoying?

MEI. Yeah, we were in turnaround, I had a backlog of thirty mortars to strip, but they insisted we spend three hours in a tent in a field, watching a play.

ČELIK. You're responding to the inconvenience, not the work itself. How did the *play* make you feel?

MEI. I… don't think I felt anything. Some girls sang, that was nice, I guess. The play was… I think it was about a teenage girl who wanted to fight beside her brother. So she lied about her age, and ended up winning a battle or something. But they all had these silly wooden guns – if they'd given us warning we'd've lent them actual rifles. And then a man in a wig gave a motivational speech, and the guys started heckling him to bring the singers back. It was kind of embarrassing.

ČELIK. So you did feel something – embarrassed. I don't blame you, the AFC shows are unforgivably awful – demoralised actors performing turgid scripts, written by propagandist hacks and party committees. Ticking, no doubt, every box on Mr Garmash's checklist, but missing the only one that matters: *Is it good? Does it move you? Is there truth at its core?* And therein lies the tragedy – for our Ministry and our nation. *Our truth is worth telling.* To the world at large, and to ourselves. The truth is: this country is engaged in an act of creation the likes of which this world has never seen, bringing a new society – a new *kind* of society – into being. But if we allow Garmash and his minions to stamp on every artist who shows the slightest spark of daring or originality… then who is going to listen to our truth? And who'll be left to tell it? (*A beat. Then.*) I'm sorry, I'm rambling…

MEI. No, it's um… nice. Inspiring.

ČELIK *smiles at this*.

ČELIK. What are you doing tonight?

MEI. Excuse me?

ČELIK *retrieves some official-looking, gold-embossed tickets.*

ČELIK. Bax's new play, *Field of Tears*, is opening at the People's Theatre. It's going to be quite the party. First-rate actors, a fine crew and the writing is... well, it's not perfect, but it's a hell of a lot better than what you saw in that tent. It'll be a good education for you.

ČELIK *offers her a ticket. She looks at it with trepidation.*

MEI. I... I can't, I'm sorry.

ČELIK. You have plans?

MEI. No, I... just can't.

ČELIK. You work in the arts now – you should get acquainted with your subject. They wouldn't let you strip rifles if you'd only ever used a water pistol, would they?

MEI *stares at the floor, embarrassed.*

(*A realisation dawning.*) Oh, if this is because... Mei, this invitation is purely in a professional capacity, you'll be joining a delegation from the Ministry – we won't even be sitting together if that's what you're worried about.

MEI. Oh no, that's not what I'm / worried about –

ČELIK. Look, I know some Ministries can get... venal, with their female employees. I assure you, nothing like that happens here.

MEI. No, it's not that. I've... never been to an actual theatre before. I don't have any... I don't know what to wear.

ČELIK. Oh...

MEI. Do I have to wear a hat?

ČELIK. A hat?

MEI. Like to a wedding?

ČELIK (*suppressing a smile*). No, you don't have to wear a hat, you'll only block the view of the people behind. But a wedding's not a bad reference for opening night. Whatever you've worn to a wedding should be fine.

MEI. I wore my uniform.

ČELIK. Okay. Well, what you're wearing now is fine. Opening night is a bit fancy… maybe lose the blazer.

To ČELIK*'s surprise,* MEI *removes her blazer, revealing her dress underneath.* MEI*'s actions are matter-of-fact – she's simply looking for confirmation. Nonetheless,* ČELIK *can't help but take in her figure.*

Yup, great. That'll do… fine.

MEI. Then… I accept your invitation. Thank you for the opportunity, Mr Čelik.

ČELIK. You're welcome.

Short pause.

MEI. Will that be all, Mr Čelik?

ČELIK. Yes that's all, thank you, Mei.

MEI *heads for the door.*

We're seated in the stalls, but I could meet you in the…

MEI *has left the room.*

…in the foyer.

Lights fade on the scene.

The BEST MAN, *and other members of the* WEDDING PARTY, *play live music as the* BRIDE *and* GROOM *reset the stage. The* GROOM *straightens the chairs, while the* BRIDE *rearranges documents on the desk, opening scripts to the appropriate pages.*

The BRIDE *changes the flowers on Mr Čelik's desk, to show the passing of time. The* GROOM *changes clothing.*

When ready, the BRIDE *and* GROOM *look to the* REGISTRAR, *who gives them a subtle nod.*

The music concludes and the play continues.

Scene Two

Mr Čelik's office, Ministry of Culture, three days later.

MEI *enters, carrying documents under her arm. She's followed by* ADEM.

MEI. Please have a seat. Mr Čelik will be… (*Checking her watch.*) a few minutes.

ADEM. Sorry I'm early – I can wait outside.

MEI. He said to bring you straight to his office.

> ADEM *takes a seat, the same one as last time. He seems nervous.* MEI *places a jug of water on the desk, fills a glass, arranges the stationery neatly.*

ADEM. Did he… Sorry, did Mr Čelik say anything else to you about this meeting?

MEI. No.

ADEM. Okay, but did he seem… pleased, or… upset, or…?

MEI. I'm not really sure.

ADEM. Is it normal for him to take such a… personal interest in…? How many first-time writers does he actually see – twice in a week?

MEI. Just you. So far as I know.

> MEI *goes back to tidying the desk. Once she's finished, she walks back around the desk in swift, purposeful movements.* ADEM *watches her as she takes up position, standing with her back to the wall. She casts an eye down at the alignment of her buttons with the waistband of her skirt – makes an adjustment. Then stands, staring ahead, arms crossed, without leaning against the wall.*

ADEM. Infantry?

> MEI *looks at* ADEM *with surprise.*

You checked your gig line.

> MEI *looks down at her buttons.*

Hard habit to break. I still eat my food like someone's going to take it away. (*Referring to himself.*) Engineer Corps.

MEI. Armoured Corps.

ADEM. Logistics?

MEI. Gunner.

ADEM *nods, impressed.*

ADEM (*referring to himself*). Sapper. Four-Six.

MEI (*impressed*). The Green Jackets?

ADEM *nods.*

ADEM. I've been discharged two years, but I still give directions with a knife-hand. Scares the shit out of old ladies. (*He forms his hand into an open palm, chopping the air as he gives directions.*) Up the street, ma'am, take a left, then a right.

MEI *laughs.*

MEI. I always fall in step with whoever's walking next to me. Force of habit.

ADEM. Me too.

A pause.

MEI. He didn't tell me anything else about this meeting – just to bring you straight here, and make sure you didn't talk to anyone.

ADEM. Did you read my script?

MEI. No, it went straight to the Director. But maybe you impressed him, because from what I can tell around here –

ČELIK *enters briskly, interrupting them –*

ČELIK. Good afternoon, Adem. (*Nodding to* MEI.) Mei.

ČELIK *carries several scripts under his arm. He heads directly for his desk.* ADEM *stands and nods deferentially;* MEI *straightens up.*

ADEM. Good afternoon, Mr Čelik.

ČELIK. Have a seat. This won't take long.

They all sit.

So, you submitted your piece – sooner than expected. Your work's flagged to come to me personally and in light of what you've written, I'm glad that's the case. Anything you'd like to say about it?

ADEM. Um... No, I... No.

ČELIK. Then let's read an extract, shall we? Mei, join us. (*He hands* MEI *copies of the script.*) Let's go from page six. I've highlighted the relevant parts. Adem, can you read the dialogue in yellow; Mei, the orange; and I'll read the stage directions in pink.

MEI *distributes the scripts, then takes a seat.*

Whenever you're ready, start us off, Mei. Top of page six.

A pause as MEI *scans the script, confused.*

Yours are the lines highlighted in orange, at the top of page six.

MEI. Yes, sorry. Sorry.

MEI *clears her throat, begins reading. Her sight-reading is still poor.*

(*Reading.*) Why include these moments, these conversations when presumably you've overheard hundreds. Clearly you've been selective, my question is: for what effect?

ADEM (*reading*). Er. I... I guess they were the ones that stuck out in my memory.

MEI (*reading*). Stuck out why?

ADEM (*reading*). I don't know. I just kept thinking about them.

MEI (*reading*). I'm not surprised. Each of these conversations is shocking in their own way. In the course of just sixty pages we have...

ČELIK (*reading*). Mr Čelik begins leafing through the pages, casting an eye over the scenes.

MEI (*reading*)....prostitution, drug dealing, gambling, child neglect, an attempted suicide and a compulsive masturbator perforating his bowel with a chair leg up his rectum. Tell me, Adem, do you hate your neighbourhood?

ADEM (*reading*). What? No. I love my neighbourhood.

MEI (*reading*). Then why do you write about it this way?

ADEM (*reading*). Because it *is* this way.

ČELIK (*reading*). A pause as Čelik scrutinises Adem over the rim of his glasses.

ČELIK *watches* ADEM *from across the table.*

MEI (*reading*). And whom do you / blame for –

ČELIK. That's enough, thank you, Mei. We get the idea.

MEI *quietly leafs through the remaining pages of the script, bewildered.*

Last time we met, I offered you encouragement, advice, and the full resources of this Ministry – along with a promise of my personal attention. And you've responded with – a prank?

ADEM. No. No...

ČELIK. Childish mockery, parroting my own words back at me – why?

ADEM. Not mockery, no. I just... tried to do what you asked.

ČELIK. What possible interpretation of my instructions could lead to this? Writing down our entire conversation and submitting it to the Ministry as if it's a scene in a play? In fact, don't answer that – we can read for ourselves what I told you to do. It's right here on page fourteen. (*He flicks the pages, reads.*) Send me something new. Send it directly to me, I'll read it personally. Just a scene, or a fragment, a couple of pages would be fine – but make it something hopeful, something inspiring. (*Looking up from the script.*) So I ask again – why did you do this?

ADEM. I promise I wasn't trying to / mock you

ČELIK. Should I report you to the Commission for Public
    Order – as I could have done the first time we met – is that
    what you want, Adem?

ADEM. No, no, that's not… I wanted to write you a scene, like
    you asked. I read that booklet you gave me, with the list of
    forbidden words and their penalties. I swear I had no idea until
    then what kind of trouble I was in when I first met you –
    I must have had hundreds of 'red flags'. You could have
    turned me in – had me fined, imprisoned, I could be in a
    camp… sorry, a re-education programme, right now. But you
    spared me. Gave me a second chance. Your instructions were
    to write something inspiring, hopeful. Well, that gave me
    hope. So that's what I wrote.

    ČELIK *watches* ADEM *for any hint of insincerity.*

ČELIK. You're trying to tell me that this is some kind of tribute?

ADEM. Well, yeah. I mean you talked about… 'tiny acts of
    courage and kindness'. And what you did for me was… an
    act of mercy. To me, that's inspiring.

    ČELIK*'s demeanour changes – he seems taken aback by
    this.*

ČELIK. Well that's… a surprise.

    Short pause.

ADEM. I'm sorry if I offended you.

ČELIK. No, no, I just… I hadn't even considered… When you
    put it like that, I'm… flattered… Thank you, Adem.

ADEM. No – thank *you.*

ČELIK. You have, however, put me in quite a quandary.

ADEM. I have?

ČELIK. Yes. I mentioned you to Bax – he's a friend of mine, as
    you know – and as a favour, he agreed to read *The Ninth
    Floor.* And he saw the same promise in your writing that I did.

ADEM (*astonished*). Bax? Really?

ČELIK. He's agreed to spend an afternoon with you, a workshop for your new piece, which I told him you were going to submit to me. But there's simply no way we can use this – well-intended or otherwise – as the basis for a workshop. We can't even use it to teach you the principles of playwriting – structure, arcs, reversals...

ADEM. Why not?

ČELIK. Because this isn't a work of fiction, it's a transcript. I assume you were recording us – what did you use, a Dictaphone?

ADEM. No, I'd never... I've just always had a good memory for what people say.

ČELIK. Oh come on, no one's memory is this clear.

ADEM. It's just a knack I suppose. Maybe that's why I prefer to write real conversations.

ČELIK. Well, memory or no memory, I'm trying to encourage you to write a *drama*. Is there nothing else you want to write about, besides your neighbours' conversations and the ones you have with me?

ADEM. Um... I don't know.

ČELIK. You can use personal experience to inspire it – your life as a mechanic, your years as a soldier, your childhood – what sticks out to you?

ADEM. Um... I guess... Kelline?

The name 'Kelline' lands with significance in the room.

ČELIK (*surprised, impressed*). You fought in the Battle of Kelline?

ADEM. My last tour. My unit fought in the valley, three months. I sometimes thought about writing something... about what it was like.

ČELIK. Well, that's more like it! An authentic account of our country's proudest military victory. *That* we can work with! Excellent. Address it directly to me. I'll read it immediately.

ČELIK *stands,* ADEM *does the same. As they head to door,* ČELIK *pauses.*

I am going to warn you, though – to avoid any possible misunderstanding – that if what you send me is a copy of this conversation you will be blacklisted here at the Ministry. Your original play will be sent to the Commission for Public Order, and you'll face every penalty they deem appropriate. Is that clear?

ADEM. I understand.

ČELIK. Good. Don't let me down.

ADEM *exits.*

ČELIK *turns to* MEI –

Get rid of those scripts, would you, Mei?

MEI *collects the scripts and makes to exit.*

(*Pointing to a metal bin.*) No, no, in here, please. Tear them up.

MEI *begins to shred the scripts into strips by hand, placing them in the bin.*

What do you make of our Mr Nariman, Mei? Bit of an enigma, isn't he? Just when I think I've got the measure of him, he goes and surprises me. Mei?

MEI'*s attention is absorbed by a line of text on one of the pages.*

What's the matter?

MEI. Nothing, Mr Čelik.

ČELIK. Tell me.

MEI (*reading a line from Adem's script*). Mei is a poor sight-reader…

ČELIK. Well, that's… just not true. You did a fine job.

MEI (*reading*). Her performance is stilted, stumbling, sometimes mispronouncing words.

   ČELIK *draws a chair close, sits beside her.*

ČELIK. Mei, don't let it get to you. Mr Nariman can only write us as he sees us, which is a very limited perspective indeed. What you see on the page here, is not *us*. In fact, like all bad writing, it tells us far more about the writer than it does about ourselves.

MEI. But you said he was a good writer.

ČELIK. I said he shows promise. And believe me he's not the first young writer to test boundaries – he's not even the most inventive. (*A beat, then.*) Can you keep a secret, Mei?

MEI. Of course, Mr Čelik.

ČELIK. Everyone believes that Bax's first play was *The Market Trader of Unity Square*. But his *actual* first play is locked in a safe in my home. No one else will ever read it.

MEI. Why?

   ČELIK *gestures to the bin.* MEI *strikes a match, drops it into the bin, setting the script alight. She feeds pages into the fire as* ČELIK *continues –*

ČELIK. It was the story of a king, who returns from war, victorious. But his real enemies were closer to home: his own friends conspire against him, stabbing him to death, seizing power for themselves. But these murderers were short-sighted and their reign is short-lived. A true friend of the king, a loyal friend, hounds them from the city, and builds a new world order. The script was very good: great dialogue, good pace. Unsurprisingly, it was almost approved for licence – I read it only by chance, and of course I realised immediately that it was the plot of Shakespeare's *Julius Caesar*, which is / banned –

MEI. That's banned.

ČELIK. Exactly. He tried to fly it in under the radar, and almost got the damn thing touring around our schools.

MEI. No…

ČELIK. Yes, the cheek! So what should I do – report him to the CPO? But this novice was writing better dialogue than half the hacks commissioned by the Capital Grand.

MEI. So what did you do?

ČELIK. I brought him in. I talked to Bax – made him believe there was more to be gained working *with* the Ministry than against us. I've always believed that most artists have an anarchic, iconoclastic streak. Show them rules, they want to break them. Show them conventions, they want to shatter them. But if, like Mr Garmash, we simply toss them to the thugs in the CPO, then who are we left with? The box-tickers. The conventional. You don't unearth the next Picasso from a paint-by-numbers competition.

MEI *looks stricken.*

MEI. You know that… Mr Garmash has made a formal complaint about you. To the Minister. I don't know if I'm supposed to… but I thought you should know.

Short pause.

ČELIK. Mr Garmash is your Head of Department in Compliance. You'd betray his confidence, purely to warn me?

MEI. I would never normally go outside chain of command. But the way he talks, I… I think he wants to remove you from your post, Mr Čelik.

ČELIK. Oh, he wants a lot more than that. If Garmash had his way, I'd be breaking rocks in a camp – sorry, 're-education centre'.

MEI. And doesn't that worry you?

ČELIK. On the contrary, it means I'm doing my job. If he's beating me up, he's leaving my artists alone. They can't do their work with Mr Garmash waggling his baton at them –

there is no emotion more inimical to creativity than fear. So I do my best, whenever possible, to interpose myself between them. Let him lash me, and not some poor poet or playwright.

MEI. Why does Mr Garmash keep working here, if he hates artists so much?

ČELIK. Oh, he doesn't 'hate' them – he fears them. Thinks they're dangerous.

MEI *scoffs*.

MEI. But... *bullets* are dangerous. Bombs, mortar shells, tanks, machetes... But I've never seen anyone killed by a painting. Or a poem. Or a play.

ČELIK. Why do soldiers fire bullets, Mei?

MEI. Because they were ordered to.

ČELIK. Why do they follow those orders?

MEI. Because... they were trained to.

ČELIK. Why did they submit themselves to training from total strangers? Why, come to that, do they put their lives in the hands of other complete strangers – and fight with every sinew to murder other soldiers, whom they've also never met?

MEI. Because...

ČELIK. Because they were told a story. And they believe it so fiercely, they're willing to die for it. An army is a story, Mei. (*Off her look*.) It is, absolutely. It's not a person or a place or an element of the periodic table – it has no objective reality in the world. Armies are composed of individuals, who cooperate because they share a story about what they're doing and why they're doing it. A war is a story. A nation is a story. Stories are the root of all human cooperation for good or ill. We enjoy telling stories, we enjoy listening to them, which is why powerful stories have a way of spreading. And the faster a story spreads, the more dangerous it can be. Gathering hundreds of people, if not thousands, in a single place at the same time is a *very* fast way to spread a story.

MEI. You mean like… a protest rally.

ČELIK. Sure. Or a play. Any audience, inflamed by the right story, can become a mob. Any mob can become a riot, and a riot could spell the end of our story and the beginning of a darker one. That's why, even today, dissidents stage fake funerals, purely as an excuse to gather. We can try to fight them with raids, arrests, punishment – the 'Garmash Method'. Or we can take that energy – the rebelliousness, the sheer audacity – and *channel it*. Like petrol in a piston or fuel in a reactor – take a potentially destructive force and harness it for constructive ends. Set the Baxes and Narimans of the world to work – no longer tearing our national fabric, but weaving it. Renewing it. Do you see?

MEI. I… think so.

ČELIK. And speaking of Bax – where did you go after the premiere? I tried to find you in the bar, but you… you vanished.

MEI. Oh, I had to go home.

ČELIK. Straight away? You missed a good party.

MEI. Yeah, it looked like fun. I wanted to… but I didn't really know anybody.

ČELIK. You knew me.

MEI. I know, but you're… you're the *Director of the Ministry*. There were much more important people queuing up to talk to you.

ČELIK. Sycophants. A hazard of my position.

MEI. I came to find you, but you were talking to the actress, the main –

ČELIK. Aanya?

MEI. Yes. And the Minister. I didn't want to interrupt.

ČELIK. You work for the Ministry of Culture, Mei, you were there on my invitation. Aanya would have been pleased to meet you. And as for the Minister, I'd far rather talk to you than that fur-coated fool. Dresses like a dead rodent, with intellect to match.

MEI *laughs with surprise*.

So, then… What did Private Mei, from Forward Base Delta, make of her first play at the People's Theatre?

MEI. Oh… um. It was very good.

ČELIK. And…?

MEI. I liked the trees – were they real?

ČELIK. You liked the trees?

MEI. I've never seen real trees inside a building before, that was… amazing.

ČELIK. What about the story, did you like it?

MEI. Oh I knew it already, we learned that at school – the peasant uprising. So I knew what was going to happen.

ČELIK. Yes, okay, but we don't go to see *Romeo and Juliet* expecting the lovers to stay alive at the end. / We go for –

MEI. I've never seen *Romeo and Juliet*. It's / banned.

ČELIK. – Banned, yes, of course it is.

MEI. Sorry, I think I'm saying all the wrong things.

ČELIK. No, don't apologise. If the play didn't move you, it didn't move you. (*He waits to be contradicted. Isn't.*) It wasn't Bax's best work, I admit. He wrote it quickly. But let's be fair to him, what with his wife and so on – I expect you read about it – he's not in the best frame of mind. But I have a suspicion if we can get Bax and Adem together, it could be just the thing to remind Bax what it's all for – get him writing again like he used to. Have you read *The Market Trader of Unity Square*?

MEI. No, I haven't.

ČELIK *moves eagerly to his bookshelf*.

ČELIK. Oh, you must, it's a classic. (*Pulling a slender book from the shelf.*) Here. Signed by the author. (*He hands it to* MEI.) You can keep it, I have dozens. But only read it if you want to – I don't want to force it on you.

MEI (*genuinely pleased*). No, no, I'd love to. If I want to help you find… great stories, like you said, I need to be able to recognise them when I see them.

ČELIK. So you might want to join my lonely crusade? As say… Assistant Development Officer, reporting directly to me?

MEI. Very much, Mr Čelik.

ČELIK *stares at her a moment. Reaches a decision.*

ČELIK. Well in that case, I think we can safely introduce you to the true sorcerers.

ČELIK *moves to a plant pot, removing a key from inside. He unlocks a drawer in his desk and excitedly rummages inside, retrieving a worn play script. He hands it to* MEI.

MEI. This is… *Romeo and Juliet*. That's / banned.

ČELIK. Banned, I know. But you're inside the Ministry now. A privilege of your position. But I'd ask that you keep this between the two of us. I've rather spoiled the ending for you, sorry. But even knowing that, I'm willing to bet you'll get to the end and dare to believe it could turn out differently. And when it doesn't, your heart will ache, wishing it wasn't so. If you can find somewhere safe, it's much better read aloud. (*A beat of hesitation.*) Actually, here's an idea: why don't we read it together? Would you like that?

MEI.… Yes I would. Thank you.

ČELIK. Not here of course. We can't be overheard.

MEI. Oh, no, of course.

ČELIK. You could come to my house. (*Off her slightly panicked expression.*) Or we could go to the park, and read it while walking. We just need to be out of earshot of the CPO's little birds.

MEI. I like walking.

ČELIK. Then that's what we'll do. Hang on to that, but keep it out of sight. Another little secret.

MEI *looks down at her copy of* Romeo and Juliet – *a flicker of trepidation (or perhaps excitement) on her face.*

Scene Three (A)

Mr Čelik's office, The Ministry of Culture, two weeks later.

ČELIK *enters – but almost as soon as he does –*

A car horn sounds outside the auditorium – a distinctive pattern of beeps.

ČELIK *freezes. Then looks towards the other* PLAYERS, *giving a signal. Immediately the company of actors transitions back to the wedding narrative, with remarkable efficiency.* ČELIK *rips the insignia off his jacket and addresses the audience as the* REGISTRAR –

REGISTRAR. Ladies and gentlemen, that's our lookout signal. Please remain calm while we investigate – and in the meantime…

The lights come up in the auditorium. The actors swiftly change costume. The GROOM/ADEM *hurries to the entrance doors to check outside.*

…a speech from the Best Man.

The BEST MAN *rushes onto the stage, with a guitar, microphone and stand.*

BEST MAN (*addressing the audience*). I've known Joel since… well, for longer than I'd like to admit. I know the Best Man's supposed to give a big speech, but… I don't write speeches, I write songs. So, Joel and Leyla – this one's for you…

The BEST MAN *sings a song for the* BRIDE *and* GROOM –

(*Singing*.)
Oh Leyla and Joel,
Two halves of a whole ['ho-el']
Heart, body and soul ['so-el']
That's Leyla and Joel.
If only you'd stole ['sto-el']
Some birth-control ['contro-el']
You might not need
To wed at such speed
Leyla and Joel.

Oh Joel and Leyla,
Prepare to set sail-ah…

Partway though – another whistle from the GROOM/
ADEM.

GROOM (*interrupting*). Sorry, everyone, false alarm. We can
carry on.

The PLAYERS *share smiles of relief, some laughter.*

BEST MAN. Well, I've started so I'm gonna finish…

The REGISTRAR *defers – 'Be my guest'.*

(*Singing*.)
Let's all exhale-ah,
We're not going to jail-ah,
Thanks to our cover –
The fictional love o'
Joel and Leyla!

The BEST MAN *bows to applause from the audience. The*
REGISTRAR *gestures to the actors to return to the stage.*

REGISTRAR. Okay, back into position please. (*To the
audience*.) Apologies for the interruption, folks. We'll pick
up where we left off – in Mr Čelik's office, at the Ministry of
Culture, two weeks later. Thanks, everyone.

*Lights fade on the audience, as the actors change costume
and the play continues –*

Scene Three (B)

Mr Čelik's office, the Ministry of Culture, two weeks later.

ČELIK *enters, humming to himself with nervous excitement. He wheels his own chair out from behind his desk and arranges the room's chairs into a circle. Then he changes his mind, wheeling his own chair back behind his desk.*

MEI *enters.*

MEI. Morning, Mr Čelik.

ČELIK (*referring to the chairs*). Mei, what do you think – like this? Or should I sit with you all in a circle?

MEI *appraises the space.*

MEI. This is fine.

ČELIK. Or, or we could do it like this?

ČELIK *moves his chair back to join the others in the circle.*

MEI. That's good, too.

ČELIK. Yes, but which is better?

MEI. I think this is better.

ČELIK. Yes, I think so, too – more inclusive. You sit here next to me, we'll put Bax there, Adem there. Yes, that'll work. Good.

As they talk, MEI *moves around the room with relaxed ease, she has a new familiarity with the space. She retrieves a playtext hidden within her blazer. She removes the key from under the plant pot, unlocks the secret drawer in Čelik's desk, and slips the book inside. She locks the drawer, returns the key to the plant pot.*

Will you give everyone a pad of paper and pen? And make sure everybody has water.

MEI. Yep, sure.

ČELIK *adjusts the chairs, a little obsessively.*

ČELIK. Do you think they'll want coffee?

MEI. Definitely.

ČELIK (*putting the chairs back where they were*). No, I think that's right – the way we had it was right.

MEI. It's exciting.

ČELIK. Yes, it is – a proper workshop. First of many. Soon this place will be a hive of creativity – you'll walk up and down these corridors and see the next generation of writers, directors, producers all in conversation, developing new work like this.

MEI. Why hasn't the Minister agreed to it before?

ČELIK. Now that she's going to be bumped up to Minister of Commerce, she seems to have given up her lifelong mission of stamping on good ideas.

This raises a smile from MEI.

MEI. Perhaps it's because she knows you'll be taking over from her.

ČELIK. Where did you hear that?

MEI. Office gossip. Apparently she can't control her own son, never mind a Ministry.

ČELIK. You don't know the half of it. Covering up his antics is a full-time job by itself.

MEI. There was an office pool on who'd take over, but they've stopped taking bets. Everyone knows it's you.

ČELIK. It's dangerous to take anything for granted in this life, but… I hope I've managed to keep the Central Committee onside. At least, the few among them who give half a shit about the arts.

MEI. 'Thane of Cawdor, that shalt be King hereafter.'

ČELIK (*smiling*). Well remembered. Fortunately, in my case, Queen Duncan is happy to relinquish her kingdom – no stabbing required. 'These hands shall remain clean.'

They share a smile.

MEI. I'll get the coffee.

MEI exits. ČELIK rearranges Mei's positioning of the water bottles – on the chair or on the floor? His deliberations are interrupted by a knock at the door. He turns to see –

BAX (played by the BEST MAN), leaning on the doorframe. BAX wears expensive, fashionable clothes and shoes, perhaps a leather jacket over a designer shirt, suede boots.

BAX. Mornin', Cap'n.

ČELIK. Well if it isn't the National Treasure himself.

BAX. How's life in the Censor Bureau – stocked up on red pens?

ČELIK. As well-stocked as you are with red wine, I imagine.

BAX. Ooof, low blow.

BAX pulls ČELIK into a bear-hug. They're easy in each other's company, old friends.

ČELIK. Well look at you – what is this, designer? You used to come to my office wearing a tie.

BAX. You used to have a cubicle on the second floor. Times change.

ČELIK *(motioning to BAX's facial hair)*. But I'm not sure about this – did you misplace your razor?

BAX. Yeah, well, without Sara around to give me a kicking, what's to stop me looking like a bum?

Beat.

ČELIK. Well, it's good to see you out and about.

They are interrupted by MEI, returning with a tray of coffee and biscuits. BAX's eyes are on her immediately. He runs a hand through his hair.

BAX. Hi there.

ČELIK. Bax, may I introduce you – this is Mei, she's assisting me on this project.

MEI *sets down the tea tray, turning to* BAX *with a deferential bow of the head.*

MEI. It's an honour to meet you. I've very much enjoyed getting to know your work.

BAX *turns on the charm for* MEI. *He plunges his hands into his pockets in a gesture of self-deprecation. Outwardly modest in the way only a person sure of their success can be.*

BAX. Oh, so you've read my work?

MEI. Mr Čelik was kind enough to lend me your first two collections.

BAX. Shit, sorry. If I'd known, I'd have staged an intervention.

MEI. Oh no, I was very grateful. He took me to *Field of Tears* at the People's Theatre. I enjoyed it very much.

BAX. Well, that's kind of you to say, thanks.

ČELIK. She liked the trees.

BAX *and* ČELIK *share a look.*

MEI. And we're… *I'm* reading *The Market Trader* for the second time now. I think it's my favourite of yours.

BAX. The debut. Everyone loves the fucking debut.

Beat.

MEI. Would you like some coffee?

BAX. Please.

MEI. How do you take it?

BAX. Any way you're giving it.

ČELIK *shoots him a look.*

Black, three sugars.

MEI *pours the coffee, as* BAX *sits down – legs outstretched/ spread, taking up space.*

So where's our young anarchist then?

ČELIK. Should be here any minute.

BAX. That play of his – *Ninth Floor*, was it? Fucking dynamite. About as unstageable as a shit in a shoe, but it's a bloody good read.

ČELIK. If you could *not* say that in front of Adem, I'd appreciate it.

MEI *hands* BAX *a coffee. She watches as* BAX *reaches into his inside pocket for a hip flask and pours a shot of liquor into his cup while* ČELIK*'s back is turned. He winks at* MEI.

Before he gets here I think it's worth making a plan of attack. Obviously he needs the works: theme, arcs, characterisation. But he seems particularly fixated on accuracy over artistry. Honestly, I'm not sure he fully grasps what a story *is*, so if you could focus on structure for today, that would help immensely.

BAX. Sure, will do. You know me, love structure. (*He takes in* MEI*'s figure as she leans down to offer him a biscuit*.) Nothing sexier than the shape of things.

ČELIK. I think he'll find it more palatable coming from you. He admires your early work.

MEI *hands* ČELIK *a coffee cup, with a biscuit on the saucer. But immediately recalls it –*

MEI. Wait, that's got jam in it. You won't want that –

ČELIK. Oh, can I have / one of the –

MEI. Here's a chocolate one.

BAX *watches this somewhat intimate exchange of biscuits, over the rim of his coffee cup.*

ČELIK. Would you check if he's here?

MEI. Sure.

>MEI *pops the jam biscuit in her mouth and exits. After a moment –*

BAX. She seems to know what you like?

ČELIK. Who, Mei? Yes, she's very attentive.

BAX. And...?

ČELIK. And a valued employee of the Ministry, so I'd appreciate it if you'd refrain from disrupting her progress.

BAX. Hey, I wouldn't dream of taking another man's biscuit.

>*Before* ČELIK *can respond,* MEI *returns with* ADEM *in tow.*

ČELIK. Here he is – Bax, this is Adem.

>BAX *and* ADEM *shake hands.*

BAX. Bomb-thrower, good to meet you.

ADEM (*disarmed*). Hi, thank you for... It's good to meet you, too.

BAX. Loved your piece about the whores and the cripples. Filthy as a shanty sewer. Nice one.

ADEM. Uh... thanks.

ČELIK. Why don't we all sit down? Adem, would you like some coffee?

ADEM. Er, yeah, is that...? Yes please.

ČELIK. Sit wherever you like. There's no formal arrangement.

>ADEM *tentatively takes a seat, and a cup of coffee from* MEI.

Let me start by saying: it's thrilling to have you both here – all of us here together – to talk about developing Adem's new work. That's the core mission of this Ministry: to foster new voices and bold new works of art. I'm especially grateful to Bax for taking time out of his busy party schedule to join us...

BAX. Well, it's a good thing you organised it for eleven in the morning.

ČELIK. I'm joking of course, Bax is one of the most prolific writers we have.

BAX. Ah, well, mostly I'm at home gaming in my underwear.

ČELIK. I also want to thank Adem for his new scene. I'm delighted you wrote to the brief: a scene inspired by your own experiences in the Battle of Kelline. Bax hasn't had a chance to read it yet –

BAX. Sorry, mate, I meant to, but I'm snowed under with the National Book Awards – I'm judging this year. Fucking novelists, can't keep it short.

ČELIK. Not to worry, we'll read it together. And I remembered a piece that you wrote, Bax, that provides a good comparison. You also wrote about the Battle of Kelline – a one-act play for the reopening of the National –

BAX. Oh yeah, fuck, that's right, I did.

ČELIK. *Captain Fikri's Sickle*.

BAX. Ah, don't read that, we don't need to hear anything of mine…

ČELIK. Don't be embarrassed, it's a lovely piece. Let's start with it.

ČELIK *gestures for* MEI *to hand out the scripts*.

Mei, you take the Corporal; Adem, can you please play the Private; and Bax, do you want to read the Young Lieutenant? I'll read the stage directions. Okay? Great – (*Reading stage directions.*) A woodland clearing, midnight. Moonlight illuminates a small field base, hastily erected among the trees. / Tarpaulin tents strung between the branches…

BAX (*interrupting*). No, no, stop. *Stop*. This is so fucking boring.

CELIK. Don't say that, it's a beautiful –

BAX. The reading, not the writing. Reading a play is like miming a symphony. The thing's not meant to be *read*, it's meant to be *performed*. So if we're going to do this, then... what do you say we actually do it – on its feet, script-in-hand?

ČELIK (*understanding*). Oh! That would be wonderful – (*To* ADEM *and* MEI.) if the two of you are game?

MEI. Um –

BAX. Brilliant – everyone on your feet. Come on, up, up, up –

They stand.

– let's give it a go! And get rid of these for a start.

BAX *shoves aside* ČELIK*'s careful arrangement of chairs, and sets the scene using office furniture as set-dressing and props.*

Okay, upstage we have... forest. (*He flings chairs towards the back of the 'stage'.*) Pine trees strung with bivouacs and tarpaulins. (*He takes off his leather jacket, hangs it across the upturned chairs.*) Huddled beneath them, trying to keep dry, the surviving members of Delta Company – starving, exhausted, short on supplies, with no relief in sight. This is a platoon on its last legs. Down and out.

ČELIK *follows his lead – pulling off his jacket, shaping it into a tent.* ADEM *and* MEI *follow suit.*

Yeah, yeah, great. Great. (*Pointing.*) Munitions crates here. Foxholes there. Pitiful excuse for a campfire here. Then downstage, waaaay over here, we need... a barricade. (*He casts his eyes around the office, looking for something suitable.*) Barricade, barricade...

ČELIK (*indicating his desk*). Might this do?

BAX. Are you serious?

ČELIK *upends his desk with a thud – as* MEI *scrambles to save the telephone and papers.*

You are a wild man. Love it.

BAX *and* ČELIK, *grinning like mischievous schoolboys,*
bulldoze the desk towards the front of the 'stage'.

Alright, so – enemy lines that way – (*Pointing over the*
barricade.) I'm taking the night watch here, so the rest of
you can sleep. And – who's playing the Corporal?

MEI *raises her hand.*

– in your bivouac, checking rations. Oh, and you're the only
one with ammo, you're going to need a gun. Everyone look
for something Mei can use a a gun.

They root around for appropriate-looking props, perhaps
borrowing from the audience – an umbrella, a walking stick,
a rolled-up newspaper – they each make an offering.

(*Offering* MEI *an umbrella.*) Here you go – rifle. (*Off* MEI*'s*
look of skepticism.) Welcome to the theatre, darling.

MEI *takes hold of one of the offerings: a mop. Looks at it*
a moment, then… snaps it to her chest, standing to attention.
Switches her hands on the 'rifle' with crisp, precise
movements, whirling it in a silent exhibition drill – the mop
snapping to her shoulder… her hip… twirling around her
head at dizzying speed – ending with a crisp thump of the
butt into the floor, standing at full attention.

A beat – the men staring at her in mute admiration.

Fucking hell. At ease, soldier.

MEI *smiles as she stands at ease.*

Alright, so places please. (*To* ADEM.) Private, offstage with
your Captain. (*To* ČELIK.) Jan, how'd'you feel about
playing the Captain?

ČELIK. I'll give it my best.

ADEM *and* ČELIK *step down off the stage, into the*
auditorium – ADEM giving MEI a crisp salute as he passes.
MEI moves upstage into the shelter of the upturned chairs.
BAX crouches behind the barricade, training his imaginary
binoculars on the audience.

BAX. It's night. It's cold. It's hell. Aaaand – lights up.

> ČELIK *dims his office lights. Angles a desk lamp towards the barricade.*

> *For a moment, no one speaks.* BAX *slowly turns his rifle this way and that, scanning the horizon.*

ČELIK (*convincing owl hoot*). Ko-kaw. Ko-kaw.

> MEI *crawls out of the bivouac, in character as the Corporal. She yawns, stretches. Hugs her arms around her, shivering.* ČELIK *gives her a thumbs-up.*

> *She tentatively approaches the barricade and addresses the Young Lieutenant.*

MEI (*reading as Corporal*). How's the fever, sir?

BAX (*reading as Young Lieutenant*). I'm fine. Go back to sleep.

MEI. Love to, sir, but we're running low on fresh water. Do you want us to lower the rations, or risk a run down to the lake?

BAX. Good suggestion, Corporal. If you pick a couple of men, form a... Actually, no, don't do that. Too risky. We'll... We should... wait till the Captain's back. He can decide.

MEI. There's a river two clicks south, sir. If we fell back we could draw water from there.

BAX. We could, but... we're not falling back without the Captain.

MEI. Yes, sir.

> *A beat, then –*

BAX. Something else you need?

MEI. It's just, sir... the Captain's been gone two days. How long are we going to wait?

BAX. Until he gets back.

MEI. Of course, sir. But... if he doesn't?

A sound from the auditorium disturbs them – the sound of grunting, heavy breathing. MEI snaps her weapon in the direction of the sound, peering into the darkness.

BAX. What was that?

MEI. Movement in the brush, sir. Should I open fire?

BAX. I… I don't…

MEI. Should I fire, sir?

BAX. Hold your… not until we… we only have three bullets… wait…

MEI cocks her gun ready to fire, when – ADEM's voice rises out of the gloom.

ADEM (*as Private*). Don't shoot! It's me – Nesh!

ADEM is dragging something – ČELIK's prostrate body – behind him.

BAX (*to ADEM*). Nesh… Who is that – ?

ADEM. The Captain.

BAX vaults the barricade, hoisting an arm under ČELIK, helping ADEM haul him to safety.

BAX (*calling*). Medic! Fetch a medic!

ADEM. It's too late, sir, he's dead. The Captain's dead.

BAX kneels beside ČELIK – who's 'playing dead' with lolling head and wide eyes.

BAX (*reading*). No…! Captain? Captain?

ADEM (*reading*). It's no use, sir. He died yesterday.

ČELIK's head pops up as he reads a stage direction from the script in his hand –

ČELIK (*reading*). A ripple of unease spreads through the camp. Sleep-starved, half-dressed men begin rousing from their bivouacs, gathering around the Captain's prostrate body.

ČELIK*'s head slumps again – a corpse once more.*

BAX (*to* ADEM). What happened?

ADEM. Scouting an abandoned village to the north-west.
Captain said we should recce for supplies, so we raided
a farmhouse – and that's when they jumped us. Nine of
them; two of us, completely surrounded. We'd run out of
ammo the day before – only one functioning gun between us.
We were done for. But the Captain had a sickle in his belt –
he'd taken it from the farm store. And… I've never seen
anything like it… he just screamed and charged the bastards.
With a sickle! Caught one of them right in the throat. They
opened fire and I just ran. I thought about coming straight
here, but… I couldn't leave the Captain. Snuck back, they'd
just left him there on the ground. Hadn't even buried him.

BAX. What's that in his hand?

A beat. There's nothing in ČELIK*'s hands apart from the
script.*

ČELIK (*quietly*). Bugger. Er, Mei, could you – ?

MEI *grabs a coat hanger. Presses it into* ČELIK*'s hand.*

BAX. What's that in his hand?

ADEM. That's the sickle, sir. Died with it in his hand. And
now… his grip's like steel. I can't pry it out.

MEI (*reading*). What do we do, sir?

BAX (*reading*). Sorry?

MEI (*reading*). Captain's dead. You're ranking officer, sir.

ČELIK (*reading*). The Young Lieutenant looks around at the
assembled men, realising with a heavy heart that he's in
command now.

MEI (*reading*). Supplies are cut, sir, we've barely got a bullet
between us. We should fall back.

ADEM (*reading*). We can't – if we retreat, they'll take this
forest and break the line. We could lose the whole bloody
war. We've got to push on.

MEI (*reading*). How are we going to push on without ammo? You can't ask the men to do that, sir.

ČELIK (*reading*). The Young Lieutenant looks from his fallen Captain to his men, watching him closely. The Young Lieutenant hesitates, before finally reaching a decision.

BAX (*reading*). The farm store where the Cap found the sickle, what else was in there?

ADEM (*reading*). Just... farm stuff. A plough, trailers, some tools – I think I saw an axe.

BAX (*reading*). Mark it on the map. I'll take a team, volunteers only, nobody has to come.

MEI (*reading*). That's right by the enemy camp, sir, what are you going to do?

BAX (*reading*). I'm going to grab anything I can use as a weapon, and before first light, I'm raiding their camp.

ME (*reading*). But... that's suicide.

BAX (*reading*). Nesh, you and the Captain were outnumbered, surrounded. By rights you should both be dead. But, against all the odds, you survived. How?

ADEM (*reading*). The Captain, sir, he saved my life.

BAX (*reading*). The Captain charged them. With nothing but a sickle in his hand. And Nesh is alive because of it. If the Captain had run away or given up, you'd *both* be dead. It's the same with our platoon: if we wait here, if we pull back, those bastards will break the line – it'll be a massacre. But if we follow the Captain's example – attack while they're least expecting it, slow them down, buy time for the Forty-Sixth Battalion to catch us up – even if it's just a day, it'll be worth it. If we can't save ourselves... we can at least save them. And if we save them, we hold this valley. (*A pause, then.*) I'll go alone if I have to.

BAX *grabs a bag off the floor, as if slinging his pack over his shoulder.*

ADEM (*reading*). I'm coming with you, the Captain saved my life, I'd like to pay that back.

ČELIK (*reading*). For a moment, no one else speaks. The Lieutenant and the Private start to walk away.

MEI (*reading*). Wait. You're not going to get far without a spotter… So, I guess I'm coming, too.

ČELIK (*reading*). Murmurs around the camp, as one by one the other soldiers step forward to join them, grabbing their packs and rifles. The Young Lieutenant swallows back emotion.

BAX. Captain would be proud of you. I'm proud of you. And I'd like to think… in years to come… your country will be proud of you. (*Louder.*) For the Captain! For the Motherland!

ALL. For the Captain! For the Motherland!

BAX *begins singing – softly at first, but with growing confidence.*

BAX (*singing*).
The light of dawn
Shines bright upon
Our noble Motherland.

The others join the song –

ALL (*singing*).
Its crimson rays
Are hymns of praise
To our noble Motherland.

BAX *and* ČELIK *are enjoying themselves, belting out the chorus, while* ADEM *and* MEI *are a little more reserved.*

Her mountains reaching skyward
Her rivers coursing strong
We'll live, we'll strive
We'll give our lives
For the land where we belong.

They break into a round of applause – everyone clapping towards BAX, *while* BAX *humbly applauds them back.*

ČELIK. Brilliant. Absolutely brilliant. Gets me every time. What a gift of a play. Truly.

BAX. Ah, it was just a little trifle. Something for the troops.

ADEM. It doesn't say, was this the Forty-Fifth Battalion?

BAX. Yup, yeah it was.

ADEM. Wow. You were in Forty-Five?

BAX. Me? No. I was in Military Intelligence, did most of my service in the Capital. But I interviewed survivors. Quite extensively.

ČELIK. Bax is very diligent in his research.

BAX. Well, you have to be. Authenticity is everything.

ČELIK. There's something the two of you share: a commitment to detail and accuracy. But what really elevates this piece – the reason I chose it – is the grasp of dramatic structure it displays. Do you want to talk a bit about that?

ČELIK *and* BAX *share a look.*

BAX. Yeah, sure. Okay. Well… So, when I approach a story, I'm thinking: who's my protagonist, who's the hero? What are his strengths, what are his flaws? What does he want? And does he want the right thing, or is whatever he wants just another manifestation of his flaws? Is he lying to himself about anything? How does he need to change?

ČELIK. In Bax's play: the Lieutenant wants the Captain – his leader – to come back. He wants the burden of command taken off his shoulders. But what he really *needs* is to find the leader within himself.

BAX. Right, exactly. So when he suffers the setback – the death of his Captain – we see how that sends him spiralling.

ČELIK. But that setback is just the beginning. Before he even has time to grieve, he's faced with an incredibly difficult choice.

MEI. And if I may say, um, a choice between two evils.

They all look to MEI.

There's no easy answer, here. Both decisions have terrible consequences. Pushing on means certain death for his men; falling back might save them, but only at the cost of many more lives. When a character has to choose between a good thing and a bad thing, we know they'll choose the 'good thing'. All they're revealing is that they're a good person. But when a character is forced to choose between two bad things, there's nowhere to hide. They have to show us who they really are.

ČELIK *smiles with pride*.

ČELIK. Exactly, Mei. Very well put.

BAX. Gold star. Someone's being paying attention in class.

ČELIK. It's a character's choices that define him in the audience's mind. Not what he says, not what other people say about him. No matter how extreme or hopeless the circumstances, characters – human beings – always have a choice. And the choices they make reveal who they are. Do you see?

ADEM. Um, I guess…

BAX. Look, I know this might all sound like a load of prescriptive bollocks, cookie-cutter stuff. But think of it more like a recipe book. You learn the basics, then you can mess with them, experiment, freestyle. Now, as much as I liked *The Ninth Floor*, what you've got is a truckload of chilli spice in search of a dish. The meat, the bones – structure, character development. That's what makes a story sing – not who the characters *are*, but how they *change*.

ADEM. But… their lives don't change – the people in my building. We've lived there for years, nothing changes.

BAX. Yeah, I get it – that's the reality. But on a stage, if your characters don't change, your audience dozes off. Maybe lots of us are stuck, maybe all of us, but we *want* to change, right? More importantly, we want to believe it's possible to change. That's the gift of a great story: the promise that we, too, can change. Heroic stories show us we can change for

the better, tragedies warn us we can change for the worse.
But either way they give us hope – that change is possible.

ADEM *looks a little unsettled, but doesn't push back.*

ČELIK. Maybe we should stick a pin in this discussion, and read
Adem's new piece. (*Gesturing for* MEI *to hand out scripts.*)
Mei, would you please read Babyface? Bax, you read
Squawky…

BAX. Squawky?

ČELIK. I'll play the Sergeant, and Adem, you can read yourself –
Monk, that is you, isn't it?

ADEM. Er yeah, you could tell?

ČELIK. Call it an inspired guess. And since this is the same
battle, in the same valley, I assume we can use the same set?

ADEM. Er… yes. Sure. Except there weren't any barricades. It
was trenches.

An awkward moment.

BAX. Anyone got a shovel?

MEI *flips the table so it's completely upside down, legs in
the air.*

MEI. Trench.

ČELIK. Perfect. I believe I start offstage. Bax and Adem centre-
stage. Adem, would you like to kick us off?

ADEM. Okay. Sure, so, um… (*Hastily reading the stage
directions.*) Sunset. A ragged, depleted unit, dressed in
bloodstained fatigues, races to set up camp in the fading
light. Amongst them is – (*Pointing to* MEI.) Babyface –
a giant of a man with a huge beard. He's kneeling, tending to
the wounded hand of his comrade – (*Pointing to* BAX.)
Squawky – a slip of a boy, living up to his nickname by
screeching his lungs dry.

BAX *lays down where* ADEM *indicates.* MEI *kneels beside
him, 'tending' to his hand.*

(*Reading*.) Nearby, a soldier – (*Pointing to himself*.) nicknamed 'Monk' – pours water over his face, trying to wash the blood out of his eyes.

MEI (*reading as Babyface*). Doc! Doc! Anyone seen the Doc?

ADEM (*reading as Monk*). He's down the ridge. In pieces. But I grabbed his pack.

MEI (*reading*). We lost Doc?

ADEM (*reading*). Frog-mine ripped his chest apart. It was… I think it was quick.

A beat.

BAX (*reading as Squawky*). 'Scuse me – I'm bloody dying here. Any chance of a moxy?

ADEM (*reading*). Monk tosses the pack to Babyface, just as Sergeant Izadi enters, wiping a hand on his trousers.

BAX (*reading*). Good dump, Sarge?

ČELIK (*reading as Sergeant*). Bloody transcendent! I haven't shit in three days. Too many 'Biscuits, brown. Six for the consumption of.'

MEI *chuckles with recognition. Glances to* ADEM, *who smiles back.*

Any sign of the bastards?

ADEM (*reading*). Nothing yet, Sarge.

ČELIK (*reading*). Monk, Babyface, you're on next watch – twenty minutes. Grab some Go Pills from the medkit or eat coffee from your ratpacks, I don't care, but you *stay awake*. We are holding this ridge.

MEI (*reading*). With respect, Sarge, what's the point? We take the ridge, they take it back. We charge them, they charge us. We slaughter them, they slaughter us. And for what?

A beat. BAX *seems reluctant to say his next line. Throws a slightly peevish look at* ADEM. *Then takes a breath, and –*

BAX (*reading*). For the Motherland.

ADEM (*reading*). They crack up laughing, pelting Squawky
with trash.

MEI *throws a piece of rubbish at* BAX.

BAX (*reading*). 'The Motherland' can suck my appendage.

BAX *and* CELIK *share a look.*

ČELIK (*reading*). All right, Squawky, give it a rest. We all
know why we're here.

BAX (*reading*). Yeah, because some bespectacled bell-end in
a cosy room in the Capital drew a dot on a map and said
'Order them to hold that ridge.' That's all the effort it cost
him – pen, paper, dot. Then he had a cup of tea while his
batman gargled his misters.

MEI (*reading*). I'd like to take that pen and shove it so far up
his rectum I can write my initials on his kidneys.

ČELIK (*reading*). Alright, that's enough. Next man grousing
can dig us a new latrine.

BAX (*reading*). Three platoons in the attack – a hundred men.
I count... eleven of us left. They'll be setting up mortars in
the valley. First sign of daylight, they're gonna shell us six
ways to Sunday.

MEI (*reading*). Sarge said to put a sock in it, Squawky.

BAX (*reading*). We're sitting ducks, Sarge. And who's going to
reinforce us? Forty-Fifth are lying down there, cut to
ribbons. What the hell are we doing here?

ČELIK (*reading*). We're here because the Forty-Fifth trod on so
many landmines there were none left for us. And we stay
because those are our orders.

BAX (*reading*). Rousing speech as always, Sarge. What d'you
reckon, Monk? None of this seem pointless to you?

They all look to ADEM.

ADEM (*reading*). We're here because they sent us. We stay
because they'll shoot us if we don't.

They close their scripts. Nobody applauds.

ČELIK. Well. Thank you, Adem, that was… bracing. Let's break for coffee, shall we? Mei, would you top us up?

MEI *is staring down at her script.*

Mei?

MEI. What? (*Then.*) Sorry. Yes, sir.

MEI *quickly stands, visibly shaken. She busies herself pouring coffee, but her hand trembles.*

BAX. Mate, you know what I'm going to say, don't you?

ADEM. I tried to leave out the profanity. It was tough – Squawky didn't use many other words.

BAX. How much of this is real conversation?

ADEM. All of it.

ČELIK. Adem has an aptitude for recalling conversations. But we've been discussing – haven't we, Adem? – that when we write fiction, we're not going for the literal truth of things. We're trying to illuminate something deeper. Because a mirror isn't a painting.

BAX. It feels a bit like your other play, Adem. I'm seeing them chatting, grumbling, but – unless I'm missing something – their situation doesn't change from the start of the scene to the end of it. Were you planning other scenes where they'd develop in some way? Squawky's clearly lost his patriotism. But what happens next – does he find it again?

ADEM. He died. They shelled the ridge. Sarge lost a leg, me and another guy dragged him out. Everyone else K-I-A.

Beat. MEI *drops a teacup with a clatter.*

MEI. Sorry.

ČELIK (*to* ADEM). But the Battle of Kelline was a victory.

ADEM. Two weeks later. Fourteen hundred men later. I was in the field hospital by then.

A pause.

BAX. Look, that's fucking awful. But... a play, especially one you're hoping will land on the national stage... isn't a field report.

ČELIK. My point exactly. I'm sorry to sound like a broken record, but we're trying to push you beyond the surface details, to something deeper.

ADEM. But... what if the truth you want to tell *is* on the surface?

BAX. Look, if you want to complain about military strategy, write a pamphlet, not a play. Because it'll never get staged, the politicians'll never see it, and I guarantee you they won't read it. Does the Minister even read the plays we do put on?

ČELIK. The Minister only reads her own press clippings and the fashion magazines she has smuggled over the border.

BAX. Probably for the best. She wouldn't know a good play if it fucked her husband.

ČELIK. Which, I have it on good authority, half her typing pool does on rotation.

BAX *and* ČELIK *share a laugh.*

BAX (*to* ADEM). I served, I get it: I know we're not all singing the national anthem every five minutes. But the sacrifice you guys made, whether or not it means anything to you, it means something to us – the people who weren't there. We owe our lives to your sacrifice. We want to celebrate you, to thank you. The story of the Forty-Fifth, taking on a whole camp armed with nothing but sickles and pitchforks, moved me to tears when I heard it. It was a privilege to bring that story to a larger audience.

ADEM. But it's not true.

BAX. Sorry?

ADEM. It never happened.

Beat.

ČELIK. Yes it did.

BAX. Of course it did. I interviewed witnesses.

ADEM. They made it up – it's an open secret. A story they started telling everyone after their Captain was shot stealing farm supplies. They didn't want to ruin his reputation. Mei knows – right, Mei?

Everyone looks to MEI *for confirmation. She opens her mouth to speak, then closes it again. She looks at the ground.*

It was common knowledge if you served at the time.

ČELIK. It seems to have passed Mei by.

ADEM. It's not just that it *didn't* happen, it *couldn't* happen. There's no world in which you can win a firefight with a rake.

Beat. BAX *glares at* ADEM.

ČELIK. Whether it did or didn't happen, isn't the point, Adem. / The point is –

BAX. I'm not making a fucking documentary, I'm making a drama – the two are not the fucking same.

Beat.

ČELIK. Bax's play may not reflect the exact words spoken by those soldiers, or their exact circumstances, but that's not what it's for. *Inspired* by real events, Bax's piece inspires greater courage in others.

BAX. It's called 'art', mate. We're writers, not fucking Dictaphones.

ČELIK. Bax, I don't think / Adem meant to –

BAX. D'you know what? I didn't have to come here this morning. I have six commissions to finish, but I came here to do you a fucking favour.

ADEM. I didn't mean to offend you.

BAX. I'm not offended, mate, I just don't like having my time wasted. I was your age once, too. I threw bricks. But in the end throwing bricks isn't building houses. There comes a point

where you have to grow up, take out your fucking…
(*Searching for the right word, not finding it.*) cement… spade,
and put one brick on top of another. Or you're not an artist,
you're nothing. You're nobody.

BAX *stands and pulls on his jacket. As he does so, the hip
flask falls out of his inside pocket and rolls on the ground
near* ADEM*'s feet.* ADEM *picks it up and holds it out to*
BAX.

BAX *grabs the flask and storms out, leaving the others in
stunned silence.*

The lights fade on the scene.

The PLAYERS *reset the furniture and change costume for
the following scene, as music plays. They replace the desk
and chairs with a threadbare armchair. Beside it, a standing
lamp with a torn shade. A stack of car magazines, and a few
other details suggesting this is the home of a bachelor on
a budget.*

Scene Four

Adem Nariman's home, Apartment 9C, two days later.

ADEM *slouches in an armchair, a magazine open on his lap.
He eats from a bowl, a simple soup. The muffled sounds of
a television can heard through the wall.*

A knock at the door. ADEM *puts the bowl down and rises to
answer it. He's surprised to see* MEI *standing outside.*

MEI. Hello, Adem.

ADEM *looks at her, confused.*

It's… Mei, from Mr Čelik's office. Maybe you don't
remember / me –

ADEM. Of course I remember you, Mei.

MEI. Oh… (*Smiling, a little embarrassed.*) I'm sorry to bother you at home. But… um.

Beat. MEI *waits for* ADEM *to invite her in. He doesn't.*

Um, would it…? Could I please come in?

A beat as ADEM *thinks on this.*

If you're busy I can come back another time.

ADEM *steps back, somewhat reluctantly, allowing* MEI *inside. She enters the apartment, looking around with interest.*

Huh. It's just like you described it in your play… The green carpet… the faded wallpaper. It's tidier than I thought it would be. (*Pointing through the wall to her left.*) So through this wall, that's Nine-D? The prostitu… sorry, the hairdresser.

MEI *listens at the wall a moment.*

ADEM. She's not in.

MEI. Yeah, of course – if she were home we'd know, right?

MEI *smiles.* ADEM *doesn't return it.*

It's nice – what you've done with the place. Cosy. (*Pause.*) Um. Yeah, so… That workshop with Bax and Mr Čelik. That went badly.

MEI *attempts a laugh, but* ADEM *remains silent.*

I wish it hadn't gone like that. I mean, I don't think it needed to go like that. Bax overreacted. Mr Čelik was saying how these big stars are all hypersensitive to criticism – not that you were criticising him. He says a lot of the job is 'managing egos'. But… I wanted to tell you, I do think Mr Čelik will change his mind. About blacklisting you. He just has to prioritise his relationship with Bax for now, but I'm sure he'll work with you again at some point in the future. Just give him some time to cool off.

A pause as MEI *waits for a response from* ADEM. *She doesn't get one.*

He's not a bad guy – Mr Čelik. I think he's a good man,
actually. He really wants to turn the Ministry into something
great – he's always going on about how it could be a
'hothouse of creativity'. He cares about what he does, and
he's good to his staff… He's been really kind to me, giving
me scripts to read, taking me to see shows.

ADEM. I'm glad.

Beat.

MEI. This job is a huge opportunity for me. My family lives in
the middle of nowhere, down south – no electricity half the
time. I thought for sure I'd get posted back down there, but
somehow I wound up in the Capital, working in a Ministry.
And when the Director takes a personal interest in your
career, that's…

ADEM. Did he send you here?

MEI. No. No, I just wanted to… see if you were alright… after
the workshop.

ADEM. I'll be fine. Thanks for asking. Take care now.

ADEM *begins ushering* MEI *to the door, but she blurts out –*

MEI. I feel like shit, okay? For not backing you up. About
Captain Fikri's Sickle. Of course I know it's bullshit,
everyone on the front line knew it. We used to call it *Captain
Fik's Sack of Shit*. I should've said that. I'm sorry.

ADEM. It's okay. You don't need to apologise.

MEI. Yes I do. It was cowardly. And… I've never thought of
myself as a coward before. So, I'm sorry.

ADEM. Well, thanks for saying so.

A pause as MEI *waits for more from* ADEM. *But still she
doesn't get it.*

MEI. Look, alright, the truth is: I was angry with you.

ADEM. Why?

MEI. Because you… We had a guy like Squawky in our unit,
too. A joker, always mouthing off about stuff. Sarge always

telling him to button it, but we all kind of loved him, really. He was with me when the base was shelled – wall caved in on him, right next to me. I couldn't pull him out from under it without ripping him in half. I tried to lift the concrete up, almost ripped my arms out of their sockets trying – he's screaming the whole time, trying to tell me something, but my ears were ringing so badly I couldn't… (*Pause.*) So… your scene. The way the guys spoke. It reminded me of him, which reminded me of that. And I don't like to… I mean, I have nightmares about it, but… in the office I usually get a break. From remembering.

A pause.

ADEM. Do you want a drink?

MEI *looks up in surprise.*

MEI. Yes.

ADEM *moves to the kitchen counter and retrieves an unmarked bottle.*

ADEM. It's bootleg liquor, but I haven't gone blind yet.

ADEM *pours a slug of liquid into two glasses. He offers her one. They drink.*

I'm sorry I stirred all that up for you.

MEI. No, I'm not… I was angry in the moment, but not now. When I thought about why I was pissed at you, but not Bax, I realised… it's because Bax's scene didn't make me feel anything at all. Because it was bullshit. Like the stuff they used to force us to watch on tour, the shit we used to heckle. So I've been thinking – if you stop writing now, and people like Bax keep writing then… that's what we're left with. Bullshit.

MEI *drains her glass.*

ADEM. Another?

MEI *nods.*

MEI. It's good stuff, as it goes. Sweet.

ADEM. One of the guys at the garage makes it in a fuel tank. He adds a bit of honey, takes the edge off – he's got a beehive in his attic. (*Filling her glass.*) I'm his best customer – it helps with the nightmares.

They meet eyes. After a moment, MEI *tuns away and sits in the armchair, sipping her drink.*

MEI. Do you think I'm cold?

ADEM. What?

MEI. Like, uptight?

ADEM. I...

MEI. Cos when I read that conversation you wrote – transcribed, whatever – between you, me and Čelik... it sort of felt like you'd written me that way. And that was weird – I didn't recognise myself. Then you said I was a shit sight-reader –

ADEM. I didn't say you were shit –

MEI. 'Poor', then.

ADEM. Sorry.

MEI. No, it was true. But I've been practising.

ADEM. I noticed.

MEI. You did?

ADEM. Yeah.

MEI. Thanks. (*Beat.*) Anyway, it got me thinking about how I'd look if you wrote up the workshop. Worse than cold – a lapdog. Brown-noser. Is that how you'd write me?

ADEM. I'd just write down what you said.

MEI. And that's what gets me – I can't change it. Cos I said it already. Whether you write it down or not, I can't change the past, can I? It's all there in black and white.

ADEM *sips his drink, watches her.*

So what would you write now? Like, right now?

ADEM. Huh?

MEI. If you were writing this scene – us two here in your apartment – what would you say about me?

ADEM. Um… I'd say…

MEI. What?

ADEM. I'd say, Mei sits in the armchair sipping her drink.

MEI.… 'in a cold, uptight way'?

ADEM (*smiling*). No. Comfortably.

MEI *puts down her drink and stands up.*

MEI. And now?

ADEM. Um… Mei puts down her drink and stands up.

MEI *walks towards* ADEM.

MEI. And now?

ADEM. Mei walks towards Adem.

MEI *takes his glass out of his hand, puts it to one side.*

Mei takes Adem's glass out of his hand and puts it aside.

MEI *leans forward and kisses* ADEM *on the mouth. She pulls back, looks at him.*

MEI. And now?

ADEM.…Mei, uh, kisses Adem on the mouth.

MEI. And then?

ADEM. He kisses her back…?

MEI *nods, and* ADEM *kisses* MEI *back.*

MEI. And then?

ADEM. Um…

MEI *begins unbuttoning* ADEM*'s shirt.*

MEI. What am I doing?

ADEM. You want me to keep / going – ?

MEI. Uh-huh –

ADEM. Okay, er... Mei unbuttons Adem's shirt. And... and Adem... takes off Mei's jacket.

ADEM *removes* MEI*'s jacket.* MEI *kisses his neck.*

MEI (*through kisses*). And now?

ADEM. Mei... um, kisses Adem's neck...

MEI *slides down onto her knees in front of* ADEM, *and begins unzipping his fly.*

Um, Mei... Mei kneels – do, do I have to still...?

MEI *pulls* ADEM*'s jeans down around his ankles, then stands up.*

MEI. Not much of a talker, are you? Monk.

ADEM *opens his mouth to speak, but says nothing.*

I like that about you. (*Then.*) Adem pulls up Mei's skirt...

ADEM *hitches up* MEI*'s skirt.*

Kisses her legs.

ADEM *kisses her legs.*

...And lays her onto the floor, climbs on top of her...

ADEM *does as instructed.*

...He kisses her hard...

ADEM *and* MEI *kiss hungrily, she arches her back, pushing her body into his –*

A car horn sounds outside the auditorium – that distictive pattern of beeps. MEI *and* ADEM *stop what they're doing and stand up quickly, pulling on their clothes.*

ČELIK *as* REGISTRAR (*to audience*). Would the congregation please stand and join the bride and groom in swearing the Oath of Allegiance. Everyone – do please stand. You can follow along in your service sheets – you'll find the wording on page two.

The REGISTRAR *leads everyone in reciting the Oath of Allegiance.*

ALL. I hereby declare, on oath, that I will support and defend the laws of my nation against all enemies, foreign and domestic; that I will bear true faith and allegiance to the same; that I will bear arms on behalf of my country when called upon. That I will work for a country that is prosperous, strong, harmonious and beautiful. I offer my body and mind to the eternal glory of the Motherland.

A whistle from the BEST MAN. *The* PLAYERS *huddle together and speak in hushed tones. They seem to come to an agreement. The* REGISTRAR *adresses the audience –*

ČELIK *as* REGISTRAR. Apologies for the interruption. There are reports of traffic police in the area. They shouldn't have any business coming inside the building, but we felt duty-bound to inform you. We – the players – have decided to continue, but we offer you the opportunity to leave now if the risk makes you uncomfortable. If you do decide to leave – we understand, and we're grateful for your support so far.

A moment for those who wish to leave. When it's clear that everyone else intends to stay –

REGISTRAR. Okay, back into position please, we'll pick up where we left off.

An awkward moment as the actors playing ADEM *and* MEI *start to undress and arrange themselves back into position, entwined on the floor. But* MEI *stops and addresses everyone –*

MEI. Actually can we... (*To the* REGISTRAR.) can we just fast-forward to the next scene? (*To the audience.*) There was a short sex scene here... but we're just going to skip to the next scene, if that's okay? Thanks. Thank you, everyone.

A pause while the actors try to remember what comes next.

(*Signalling to* BAX.) You're up, this is your scene.

BEST MAN/BAX. Oh shit, yeah...

The BEST MAN *gets into position ready to play* BAX, *while the others dress the stage for the next scene: a cheap hotel room, single bed, a small writing desk covered in papers. The surfaces are strewn with empty liquor bottles, street-food cartons and ashtrays filled with cigarette butts and chewing gum.*

When everyone is ready, the lights change and the play continues with a knock at the door.

Scene Five

A bedroom in a cheap guesthouse, one week later.

A single bed, a small desk and chair. Two open suitcases on the floor, spilling clothes. The curtains are drawn, the room lit by a small desk lamp.

BAX *lies asleep on the bed, tangled in a mess of bedclothes and loose pages of script – he clearly fell asleep reading. A loud rap at the door stirs* BAX *from sleep, he jolts awake.*

BAX. C-coming...

BAX *drags himself out of bed, accidentally treading in last night's dinner as he goes. Another rap at the door.*

Yes, alright, Mags, keep your hair on! What is it this time – ?

BAX *wipes his bare foot on the carpet and answers the door, to* ČELIK.

Jan...? I thought you were the landlady. What are you doing here in the middle of the night?

ČELIK. It's lunchtime.

BAX. Oh. Right...

BAX *slopes back into the room, a little self-conscious.* ČELIK *follows him inside and watches as* BAX *attempts to kick aside some of the mess, closing the suitcases, picking up dirty dishes.*

ČELIK. I've been worried about you. Haven't heard from you all week, then you didn't show up to the Nominees' Dinner...?

BAX. I didn't feel up to it.

ČELIK. Did you get my messages? I thought your phone was broken, I went by the house...

BAX. Yeah, well, I don't live there any more.

ČELIK. So I discovered. Since when?

BAX. Since... Sara. Place just reminds me of her. Smells of her, all those chemicals, makes me queasy.

ČELIK. Then have it cleaned.

BAX. Pipes are blocked. Power's out. Whole place is a fucking shell. (*Reaching for a bottle of liquor.*) Drink?

ČELIK. No, thank you.

BAX. I'm having one.

BAX *pours himself a generous drink, his hand trembling slightly.*

ČELIK. Your neighbour told me you were here. Honestly, I struggled to believe her.

BAX. It's not as bad as it looks – there's an ice machine. The toilets flush, most days.

ČELIK. Bax, this is not a place befitting a man of your stature, why not stay somewhere... nicer?

BAX. Broke, aren't I? (*Then.*) Sara was in so much pain towards the end – I was giving her horse tranquillisers. Not cheap.

ČELIK. Why on earth didn't you tell me?

BAX. Tell you what? I ran up colossal debts smuggling ketamine into the country?

ČELIK. I wouldn't have told anyone. I would have helped.

BAX. Yeah? You'd've shoved bags of pills up your rectum?

ČELIK. That wouldn't have been necessary. I could have called customs, arranged an import licence – on behalf of a friend.

BAX. Is that what you are – a friend?

ČELIK. Of course. (*A beat. Then.*) I'm going to make some calls. Put you up somewhere proper.

BAX. Lucky me. Another scrap from the king's table?

Beat.

ČELIK. What's gotten into you?

BAX *picks up the loose pages of script from his bed, and hands them to* ČELIK – *who looks them over, a realisation dawning –*

He didn't…

BAX. The workshop we had with him. In ten glorious pages. Plus some conversations he had with you.

ČELIK. That… little shit. He's blacklisted at the Ministry, can't send this drivel to me, so now he's pestering you.

BAX. At first I couldn't fathom what the fuck it was. Why's he sending me transcripts of conversations he had with you? But then I got to the bit about our workshop, and realised what he'd done.

ČELIK. A childish prank.

BAX. No, no – I mean I realised what *we'd* done.

ČELIK. Bax… you can't let the scribbled ravings of a car mechanic upset you. (*Indicating the script.*) This is a hatchet job. Distortions and lies.

BAX. That's what I thought, too: he's just taking the piss. (*Pointing to a page in the script.*) Look here, '…Bax is outwardly modest, in the way only a person sure of their success can be.' He's calling me an arrogant twat. Then I'm reading through the dialogue, thinking: we didn't say half of this, he's made us sound like a pair of bloviating cunts.

ČELIK. Exactly, it's a caricature.

BAX. But. Then I read it again. That play I wrote, *Captain Fikri's* cocking *Sickle* – did you let him leave with a copy? Cos we never published the thing, did we?

ČELIK. Of course not – I blacklisted him and sent him packing.

BAX. That's what I thought. Thing is, he's got it word-for-word. I compared it with the real thing – (*Reaching for the original play script to show* ČELIK.) Look. The guy's got a memory like nobody I've ever known. So then I read the whole thing again. And again. And again, and... I did say that. All of it. So did you. That's not a caricature – that's *us*.

ČELIK. No it isn't –

BAX. Bloody is. Look at it.

ČELIK *tosses the script aside.*

ČELIK. I don't need to look at it. So what if we said some of those things – we were trying to help him.

BAX *pours himself another drink, turns these words over –*

BAX. 'Help him...'? Hmm. Here's this guy, writing down what he sees around him, how we talk, how we act, how things are. And we're trying to tell him that isn't art.

ČELIK. Because it isn't.

BAX. No? Maybe if we ever actually talked about how things are – I mean *ever* – we'd need our fiction to reach for something more. Sorry, something 'deeper' – that's your favourite word, isn't it? But when we're performing a fiction every day... pretending we don't see what we see, pretending we don't think what we think, know what we know – when that's how all of us live, all the time... the last thing we need is *more* fiction. Maybe the urgent truth is the one right in front of our noses? (*A beat.*) You're the one who yammers on about 'art' and 'truth' on the 'national stage'. (*Gesturing to Adem's script.*) There's your truth. Put it on.

Beat.

CEILK. Alright. I see what's happened: you've been sitting in the dark for days on end, drinking and obsessing over this – losing all perspective. We need to get you out of this room – (*He picks up the script.*) and get this out of your head. I'm going to toss this in the furnace, and then we'll –

BAX (*leaping up*). Don't you dare.

BAX *snatches back the script – shocking* ČELIK *with his fervor.*

ČELIK. I'm going to put that down to the alcohol.

BAX (*thumbing through the script*). Where is it…? The bit where you first tell him about me. About us. Waving my name around like a trophy. Adem says the same thing everyone says, everywhere I go: he loves *The Market Trader.* They all love *The Market Trader.* I can't shake it off. First play, never lived up to it again.

ČELIK. That simply isn't true. You've done extraordinary work.

BAX. I *did* extraordinary work. Then I met you.

Beat.

ČELIK. Alright, you want the truth? Yes, *Market Trader* is your best piece. By a country mile. Yes, you've gotten lazy, repetitive and complacent. But don't try to pin your decline on me. The drinking, the drugs, the actresses – I didn't do that. You did. And you loved every decadent second of it. My crime, if I committed one, was putting you on that pedestal, by putting your work in front of thousands of people. As I would have done for Adem if he hadn't pissed away the opportunity.

BAX. And what does that say about us? When men like you have power over men like him.

ČELIK. Would you rather have 'men like me', or men like Garmash? That's the real choice here.

BAX. At least Garmash is honest. People make art, he hates it, he smacks them in the face with a fucking baton. Everyone knows where they stand. What you do is… *so* much more insidious. He thumps people. You… seduce them. He rips chunks out of scripts. You rip chunks out of people. (*Correcting himself.*) No, no, that's not true – you convince us to rip chunks out of ourselves. A scrap of heart here. Sliver of spleen there. That bit of brain at the front, that's going to have to go. We chop and we slice, saw through our bones, hack off whole limbs – to fit your idea of who we need to be. And I'd gotten so used to functioning without them – all the parts of me you'd chipped away – I barely remembered what I'd lost. Until I saw myself through Adem's eyes – the… mutilated marionette you've made of me. And I've been drinking ever since.

A short pause.

ČELIK. If you want to marinate in filth and self-pity, you go ahead. But when the fever breaks, which it will, when you remember who your friends are… you know where I am.

BAX. Sure. I know where you are. (*Then.*) For now.

Beat.

ČELIK. What does that mean? 'For now'…

BAX *searches the bedsheets for a missing page of script. Finds it. Hands it to* ČELIK.

BAX. Cover page.

ČELIK. What…? (*Reading.*) *A Play*, by Adem Nariman… and Jan Čelik.

BAX. You're a writer now. Congrats.

ČELIK. How fucking dare he…

BAX. You want to be careful who else sees that. Some pretty choice phrases you've got in there for your boss. If he sends it in –

ČELIK. He wouldn't… He couldn't, we blacklisted him.

BAX. Yeah, and he always respects your instructions.

ČELIK. Where's your phone?

BAX. Time to lock the stable door?

ČELIK urgently scans the room, locating a shabby phone. He lifts the receiver, attempts to dial. Bangs his fingers on the switch hook.

ČELIK. Why doesn't your phone work?

BAX. Takes coins.

ČELIK. Fuck.

ČELIK hurriedly pats himself down, fumbling in his pocket for coins. He feeds the meter, picks up the phone to dial, but –
BAX places a finger on the switch hook, blocking the call.

Remove your hand.

BAX. No.

CELIK. There are other artists under my protection: sculptors, film-makers, poets. One of those artists is you, lest you forget.

BAX. And if I don't want your 'protection' any more?

CELIK. Then you are welcome to discover what life is like without it.

A pause. Then – BAX *lifts his finger off the switch hook. Takes up the bottle. Slinks back to the bed for a swig.*

CELIK *dials.*

Hello, operator, this is Director Čelik, I need you to connect me to the Commissioner please… Yes I know this is an outside line. Tell him it's Jan calling, tell him it's urgent.

Lights fade on the scene. The actors playing ČELIK *and* BAX *leave the stage, while others change the scenery. The bedroom furniture is replaced by a desk and two chairs.*

Lights come up on –

Scene Six

A police interrogation cell, the following day.

A table and chairs. A low-hanging ceiling light illuminates
MEI, *her hands cuffed to the table. Her hair is loose,*
dishevelled. She's dressed only in Adem's shirt – the one we saw
him wearing in Scene Four – now stained and torn.

A paper cup of water rests on the table, just out of MEI's *reach.*
She tries to drink from the cup by craning her head over it,
lifting it with her teeth, but… it spills. She curses under her
breath, presses her face to the table, and slurps a few precious
sips of water off the surface.

The sound of metal bolts unlocking, and – ČELIK *enters the*
room. MEI *straightens up immediately, overcome with relief.*

MEI. Mr Čelik, thank god you're here! I don't know what the
    hell's going on. I've been here for hours –

ČELIK. Why were you there?

Beat.

MEI. Why was I – ?

ČELIK. At his apartment – what were you doing there?

MEI. We… were talking. They kicked the door down, barged
    in – four, maybe five of them – they turned his flat upside
    down and –

ČELIK. But why? Why were you talking in his apartment?

MEI. I went to see him after the workshop. I was worried he
    might be / upset –

ČELIK. The workshop was a week ago.

Beat.

MEI. Why's he been arrested? The CPO ripping his home apart –

ČELIK. I'm sure they had their reasons. I'm interested in yours.

MEI. The warrant was from the Ministry. *Our* Ministry.

ČELIK. You aren't answering my question.

MEI. You aren't answering *my* question – why was he arrested?

ČELIK. Because he's a criminal and that's what happens to criminals. Why were you there – ?

MEI. What was his crime? He was in his own home / minding his own –

ČELIK. Where are your clothes?

Beat.

MEI. They wouldn't let me… There wasn't time to…

A short pause as this lands on ČELIK. *He sinks into a chair.*

ČELIK. Was this the first time?

MEI. Could we talk about this… somewhere else?

ČELIK. How many times? When did it start?

MEI. Is it a crime to have a personal / life?

ČELIK. To fuck a political dissident when you work for a Government Ministry – yes, it's a crime. It's about ten different crimes!

Pause.

MEI. You called them 'thugs'.

ČELIK. Is that his shirt?

MEI. You said we weren't that kind of Ministry.

ČELIK. Why…? Why *him*?

MEI. I… I'm sorry if you… if you thought that we…

ČELIK. You came to my house. You met my sister. (*Beat.*) What could he possibly offer you? Look where he's landed you!

MEI. Adem didn't call the CPO. (*Beat.*) Why did you do it?

ČELIK. Why did *I* do it?

MEI. Why did you loose the dogs on him? You know they broke his hands – ?

ČELIK. He broke the law. Repeatedly.

MEI. In the car door. Held him there and slammed it shut.

Beat.

ČELIK. The CPO have their methods. I have no control over those. Adem had a chance to deal with me, he threw it back in my face.

MEI. You're scared of him. Aren't you.

ČELIK. Don't be ridiculous.

MEI. Why? You're about to be a Minister, he's a mechanic – why are you so threatened by him?

ČELIK. It's not *me* he's threatening, it's everything I'm trying to build –

MEI. Which is what, exactly? Artists who suck the teat get a house, the ones who don't get their fucking hands broken?

ČELIK. Listen to yourself, Mei. You're not a student, you're a public servant in handcuffs. You are right on the edge of a fucking abyss. And you have no notion how deep it is. *He's* not going to pull you out of it.

MEI. And you are?

ČELIK. There are police reports, Mei, CPO records. I can't make that go away. When I'm Minister, maybe… I could find a way to bring you back in. If I wanted to. But right now, your best-case scenario is walking out of here intact. And your worst-case… is a lot worse than I think you realise.

Beat.

MEI. Do you want me to beg?

ČELIK. Of course I don't want –

MEI. Bat my eyelashes, drop to my knees?

ČELIK. A little acknowledgment of the risk I'd be taking, the capital I'd be burning, by letting you walk out of here.

MEI. So you *do* want me to to beg? Is that Adem's real crime –
being ungrateful for the handouts from the great Director
Čelik?

ČELIK *approaches* MEI. *She shrinks back in fright. He
leans in close, until they're almost touching, then – unlocks
the handcuffs tethering her to the table. He steps away.* MEI
stands a moment clutching her sore wrists.

Thank you.

ČELIK. The Booking Officer has your clothes. End of the
hallway on the right.

MEI *moves to exit, pauses by the door.*

MEI. What about Adem?

ČELIK *doesn't respond.* MEI *exits.* ČELIK *stands a moment
before turning to the doorway and calling out to the guards.*

ČELIK. Send him in.

ČELIK *takes a breath, composing himself for –*

Scene Seven

A police interrogation cell, minutes later.

ADEM *sits at the table across from* ČELIK. *He wears a prison-
issue shirt and trousers, no shoes. His bloodied hands are
bound with dirty bandages. His hands are fastened to an anchor
point bolted to the tabletop.*

ČELIK *retrieves Adem's script from his inside pocket. He unfolds
the pages – they are worn, crumpled, well-read. He pushes the
script across the table towards* ADEM.

ČELIK. It appears I'm your co-writer now.

ADEM. So many of the words were yours, I couldn't claim all
the credit.

ČELIK. Don't do that.

ADEM. Do what?

ČELIK. Don't pretend this parody is anything like an accurate representation of what passed between us.

ADEM *doesn't respond*.

If you're on some kind of suicide mission then that's your business – but did you have to drag Mei down with you?

ADEM. How is she?

ČELIK. You don't deserve to know.

ADEM. I had no idea the CPO were coming.

ČELIK. The minute you put my name on this piece of poison and sent it to Bax, you knew full fucking well the CPO were coming. You didn't leave me any choice.

ADEM. I thought 'we always have a choice'.

ČELIK (*angry*). Don't you quote… (*Mastering himself.*) I didn't come here to debate aesthetics.

ADEM. Why did you come here?

Beat.

ČELIK. I want to know when it happened. I've read and reread these pages dozens of times, and I still can't work out… When was it? What did I do to offend you? All I ever tried to do was help you. Encouraged you, championed you, tried to change your life. What was the moment when you decided to throw all that away and instead – try to destroy me?

ADEM. There was no 'moment'.

ČELIK. So this was your intention from the beginning.

ADEM. No. I don't want to destroy you.

ČELIK. Then why portray me like this? (*Tapping the script.*) You've reduced me to thirty pages of preening, pontificating, hypocrisy. And that is not who I am, it just isn't. I plant the

flowers I can, on hostile soil, and I nurture them, protect
them, with every fibre of my being, from hordes of people
who would trample them. And yes, that involves constant
negotiation, picking my battles extremely carefully because
those people have power and they would trample me, too, in
a heartbeat, and there will be no more flowers. When I look
at *you* in these pages, do you know what I see? A stubborn
child. Spurning advice, pouting on the sidelines and judging
the people brave enough to actually play the game, with all
the mess and struggle that entails. Maintaining your precious
purity, at the cost of having no power whatsoever to change
anything. Because there are no pure things on this earth. You
parrot the words we say, transcribe our transgressions, but in
the end *you* are the one who refuses to see things as they
really are. Compromise is not corruption. I'm trying to build
a… Trojan horse to smuggle true art into this country and
you want to smash it to bits and show everyone what's inside
before they've opened the gates. For what?

ADEM. I had three conversations with you. I wrote them down.
Now I'm here.

ČELIK *slams the table, furious –*

ČELIK. Because you put yourself here! This is not my fault, the
Ministry's fault, the CPO's fault – this little drama, you made
for yourself. When you jump out of a window, you can't
blame the concrete for the consequences.

ADEM (*looking at his hands*). They've been in twice today.
Slammed my hands in the cell door. I think it stops the bones
from setting.

ČELIK. Do you want me to feel sympathy for you? Guilt?

ADEM. I'm just telling you what happened.

ČELIK. Well, let me tell you what happens next. You're going
to the camps, I'm going home. You'll quarry stones in the
freezing cold, until your body gives out. I'll be appointed
Minister for Culture. You'll die in obscurity, unmourned, in
an unmarked grave. I'll nurture new artists, new voices.

Their work will be enjoyed by millions, while *your* work –
(*Indicating Adem's script.*) will be seen by no one. Never
staged, never read, never watched. So I hope you enjoyed
your petty act of vandalism. I hope it was worth it.

ČELIK *stands to leave.*

ADEM. I expect they'll break my hands again, when I get back
to my cell. You could watch, if you like. Or save them the
trouble, do it yourself.

ADEM *offers his hands to* ČELIK.

ČELIK. You'd love that, wouldn't you? (*Indicating the door.*)
Drag me down to their level. 'See? I was right all along. Mr
Čelik is nothing more than a thug.' Unfortunately for you,
I am a lot more than that. And I will not let you diminish me,
with your cheap provocations –

ADEM. If you need other people to do your violence for you,
are you 'more' than a thug? Or less than one?

ČELIK *clenches his fists, angered by this. For a moment he
looks ready to strike* ADEM. *But he reins in the urge.*

ČELIK. I won't rise to this. I am not who you say I am. I'm not
your enemy, and I never was –

SLAM! The entrance doors to the venue burst open. Armed
CPO AGENTS *storm the room, led by* SERGEANT
PETROV. *There's no time for the* PLAYERS *to scramble
back to the wedding narrative.*

SERGEANT PETROV (*to the audience*). Everybody stay in
your seats! Hands in plain sight. No sudden movements.
Don't even think about trying to leave.

The PLAYERS *hurriedly adjust their costumes, as the* CPO
AGENTS *march towards them.*

ČELIK *as* REGISTRAR. Officers, welcome. How may we help
you?

SERGEANT PETROV. Stay where you are, hands where I can
see them. (*To* BAX.) You as well. (*To* MEI.) And you.
Nobody move.

ČELIK *as* REGISTRAR. Officers, this is a licensed wedding.

SERGEANT PETROV. Step aside please.

ČELIK *as* REGISTRAR. I can show you our registration, the certificate –

SERGEANT PETROV. I said stand aside!

ČELIK nods and steps aside.

ČELIK *as* REGISTRAR. Everyone, stand back and let the officers go about their business. Hopefully they'll be on their way shortly.

A CPO AGENT grabs a box of props and costumes from the side of the stage, upturns it.

Please be careful with that, we have some entertainment planned for the reception –

A SENIOR OFFICER arrives in the doorway. He calls up the aisle to CPO AGENTS.

SENIOR OFFICER. Stand down, Petrov.

The actors turn towards the SENIOR OFFICER. He is dressed differently to the CPO AGENTS. He wears a three-piece suit with government insignia, denoting a senior rank. On closer inspection, it has much in common with the costume worn by ČELIK (though much more expensive-looking). This man is the REAL ČELIK.

The PLAYERS recognise him. Watch in silence as he walks slowly up the aisle towards them.

REAL ČELIK (*to the* OFFICERS). No need for physical evidence on this one. The certificate's forged, the wedding's a sham… (*He takes in the audience.*) And we're not short on witnesses.

REAL ČELIK reaches the top of the aisle and approaches the platform.

Hello, Mei.

MEI (who is in fact the real MEI) looks at REAL ČELIK with trepidation.

It's good to see you again.

A short pause. REAL ČELIK *tears his gaze away from* MEI, *back to the audience –*

Ladies and gentlemen, I apologise. We won't drag this out, but we will need your identity cards and you will – *all* – need to answer some questions. My associates – (*Gesturing to the* CPO AGENTS.) will be minding the doors, in case anyone thinks of leaving prematurely.

The CPO AGENTS *block the doors.* REAL ČELIK *steps towards the platform, stopping to scrutinise* BAX (*who is in fact the real* BAX).

BAX. Čelik.

REAL ČELIK. Bax… what on earth are you doing here?

BAX. Penance.

REAL ČELIK. You look thin.

BAX. Fewer canapés on the underground theatre scene. And less claret.

REAL ČELIK. I don't doubt it. (*Indicating their surroundings.*) Bit of a step down from the Grand Central, don't you think?

BAX. Or a step up.

REAL ČELIK *considers replying. Decides against it. Turns instead to come face to face with –* ČELIK.

REAL ČELIK (*comparing himself to* ČELIK). Not bad… the boots, the handkerchief. The blazer's a little boxy, but the colour's good. One crucial difference though. (*Holding up his own ungloved hands.*) No leather gloves. I don't wear them, never have, they make me sweat. (*To* ČELIK.) I don't suppose you can even take them off yourself. Shall I help you?

ČELIK *refuses help. Instead uses his teeth to remove his gloves. His hands make for a gruesome sight – scarred, deformed, the fingers crooked into claws.*

From now on, ČELIK *will be referred to as the* REAL ADEM.

(*To audience, gesturing to* REAL ADEM.) Adem Nariman,
by the way. Ten points to you if you worked that out for
yourself. But if you're playing *me*... who have you roped in
to play *you*?

REAL ČELIK *looks around, settling his gaze on the*
GROOM/ADEM.

(*To* ADEM, *with surprise*.) Hari? (*Almost laughing at the
notion*.) Oh, Hari, you absolute wally. What will your mother
say this time? (*to the audience*) Ladies and gentlemen, the
wayward son of our long-suffering Minister for Culture.
Disappointing his parents yet again.

The actor playing ADEM *is actually* HARI, *the Minister's
son.*

HARI. I didn't choose my parents. I don't support their politics
and I –

REAL ČELIK (*sharply*). Shut up, Hari. You may be a Minister's
son, that doesn't make you important. Go wait in my car, I'll
deal with you later.

HARI. I'm not going anywhere with you.

REAL ČELIK. You can face your mother, or you can face the
courts, then the camps. The choice is yours.

HARI. I'm with them.

HARI *turns away from* ČELIK. *Moves to stand beside*
REAL ADEM.

REAL ČELIK. We'll see. (*Then, to* REAL ADEM.) Aged
yourself down a bit, haven't you. Is that how you see
yourself? Young, handsome, muscular. I thought you were all
about 'the truth', 'seeing things for what they are'. Seems
you have an ego after all. Is this what floats your boat –
watching your girlfriend cop off with a younger man, in front
of a crowd of strangers?

REAL ADEM *adjusts his stance, absorbs the blow.*

(*To the audience*) Does that take the sheen off a bit? You
were rooting for the young lovers, now you have to imagine

her – (*Pointing to* MEI.) with *him* – (*Pointing to* REAL
ADEM).

REAL ČELIK *opens his jacket pocket, removing a rolled-up*
script – dog-eared and well-worn. He points it towards MEI.

You've been a bit selective in your contribution, haven't you,
Mei? Every word that passed between Adem and me is in
this script but there's a great deal between the two of *us* that
seems to be missing. (*Turning to the audience.*) Scenes You
Didn't See. Mei and Director Čelik take long walks through
Monument Park. Mei and Director Čelik enjoy languid
dinners in the New District. All those late nights in my living
room, reading illicit literature and discussing the meaning of
art, life… love.

REAL ČELIK *looks to* MEI. *She meets his gaze.*

MEI. You were kind to me. I'm grateful for that. But you never
wanted a partner. You wanted a parrot.

A beat, as REAL ČELIK *is momentarily stymied.*

REAL ČELIK. Did you honestly think I wouldn't catch up with
you, eventually? (*Addressing all the* PLAYERS.) Did you
think you could keep performing this travelling clown show –
in town after town, night after night? Surely you knew this
moment would come.

REAL ADEM. We knew. But now that it's happened… I'm glad
it's you.

REAL ČELIK. Because you want to rub it in my face?

REAL ADEM. Because it needs an ending.

REAL ČELIK. There really is no limit to your vanity, is there?
It's a black hole – (*Indicating the other* PLAYERS.) you've
sucked all of them into it. And you really couldn't give a fuck.

REAL ADEM (*indicating the script*). We'd got as far as Scene
Seven. It was your line. 'I won't rise to this.'

REAL ČELIK. As true now as it was then.

REAL ADEM. But we could pick up from the top of page
seventy-two, if you like. 'Your work will be seen by no one.
Never staged, never read, never watched.'

Beat.

REAL ČELIK (*quoting*). Well, let me tell you what happens
next. You're going to the camps, I'm going home.

REAL ADEM. You were half right.

REAL ČELIK. And I've been longing to ask you about the
other half. In the entire history of our nation's penal system,
exactly one prisoner transportation van has had a wheel fall
off – literally fly off the axle – while en route to the camps.
And it just so happens that this one van – which rolled into
a field at sixty miles an hour, rendering the driver and the
prison guards unconscious, allowing all prisoners on board
to escape – was the van carrying Adem Nariman. Aspiring
playwright and actual car mechanic.

REAL ADEM. You think I sabotaged the van.

REAL ČELIK. I know you sabotaged the van. You loosened the
wheel nuts.

REAL ADEM. Firstly, we call them lug nuts. And secondly –
I didn't loosen them.

REAL ČELIK. Come on, Adem, your commitment to truth is
legendary. Don't start lying now.

REAL ADEM. I'm not lying. I didn't loosen the lug nuts.

REAL ČELIK *scrutinises* REAL ADEM. *Lets it go.*

REAL ČELIK. You could have disappeared into the cornfields.
And never looked back.

REAL ADEM. That's exactly what I did.

REAL ČELIK. And yet somehow you found the time… and the
paper… and the *postage*… to send a copy of this –
(*Brandishing the script.*) to the home address of the Minister
for Culture.

BAX. Actually that was me. With some help from a friend.

HARI. He means me.

BAX. I do, in fact, mean him.

REAL ČELIK. And against all odds – for the first time in her seven-year tenure – the Minister of Culture decided to sit down and read a play.

REAL ADEM. You should be flattered.

REAL ČELIK. I was fired. My ministerial career cancelled before it began. I lost my job. My home. Forced to move in with my mother.

MEI (*softly*). 'The slings and arrows of outrageous fortune.'

REAL ČELIK *looks to* MEI *and smiles* –

REAL ČELIK. But then, at my lowest ebb, I received a phone call. From the Minister of Justice. He, like everyone else, had read your script. He wanted to know if it was true – if I'd really said all those things. And I told him, 'No, sir, this play is a lie.' And replied, 'Well that's a shame. Because we're about to open the new Central Court in the People's Palace of Justice. We're planning to experiment with allowing the public to watch justice being done. And the man in this script – a man who understands that it is not the literal, surface truth of things that matters, but the deeper truth they reveal; a man who believes that the right story, told the right way, can elevate, educate and inspire the public to an ever-deeper devotion to their Motherland... Well, that's the kind of man we need.' And I said, to the Minister for Justice: 'Sir, every word of this script is precisely and profoundly *true*.' Which is why, as of this morning, you are looking at the newly minted Director for Public Prosecutions. And my first act in my new post – my opening season, if you will – shall be the Trial of Mr Adem Nariman. Fugitive prisoner. Dissident playwright. And serial child-molester. Who has travelled the length and breadth of this country – leaving a trail of traumatised little boys in his wake.

REAL ADEM. So it's like that. Show trials.

REAL CELIK. Every trial is a show. And let me tell you, the new Central Court is a glorious auditorium. The public galleries alone can seat up to five hundred people. With cameras installed to broadcast the – edited – highlights on television, every night. You may have ridiculed me in front of – (*Gesturing to the audience.*) a few hundred people. But I will eviscerate you in front of millions.

Silence.

Well? Nothing to say? We're about to stage the greatest drama this nation's ever seen.

A beat.

REAL ADEM. The thing about lug nuts is –

REAL ČELIK. I think we're way past lug nuts –

REAL ADEM. *The thing about lug nuts is* – when they're too loose, it's not much of a problem. The wheels wobble a bit, rattle around, but you get plenty of warning that something's wrong. The danger comes when you screw them down too tight. Put them under more stress than they can bear. That's when they crack with no warning whatsoever. It's a common mistake, thinking the tighter you lock everything down, the harder you wrench things into place, the safer you'll be. When the reality is you're just hastening the catastrophic collapse of the system. One day, without warning, the wheels come off. And from there, you're in the hands of the forces you can't control. (*A beat. Then.*) You have to know the breaking point of things.

A beat.

REAL ČELIK. I'd save the speeches for the courtroom, if I were you. (*Then.*) Well, I think that's the curtain, don't you? (*To* SERGEANT PETROV.) Them in the van.

CPO AGENTS *escort the* PLAYERS *from the room, as* REAL ČELIK *address the audience.*

Ladies and gentlemen, take a good look at the people to your left and right – odds are they'll be your cellmates tonight. Stay in your seats until called by an officer, we'll start with Row A and work back from there. Have your identity cards ready for confiscation. If you resist, we will shackle you. If you speak, we will silence you. That's it. The end. Lights down. (*A moment, then.*) Lights down!

The End.

adies and gentlemen,
left and right holds ar
Stay in your
Row A

ALMEIDA
THEATRE

The Almeida Theatre makes brave new work that asks big questions: of plays, of theatre and of the world around us. Whether new work or reinvigorated classics, the Almeida brings together the most exciting artists to take risks; to provoke, inspire and surprise our audiences.

Since 2013, the Almeida has been led by Artistic Director Rupert Goold and Executive Director Denise Wood.

Recent highlights include Associate Director Rebecca Frecknall's Olivier Award-winning production of *A Streetcar Named Desire*, featuring Patsy Ferran, Paul Mescal and Anjana Vasan; Rupert Goold's productions of *Tammy Faye*, a new musical from Elton John, Jake Shears and James Graham; Peter Morgan's *Patriots* and Steven Sater and Duncan Sheik's musical *Spring Awakening*; Danya Taymor's production of Jeremy O. Harris' *"Daddy"*; and Yaël Farber's production of *The Tragedy of Macbeth*.

Previous productions include Rupert Goold's Olivier Award-winning productions of James Graham's *Ink* (transferred to the West End and Broadway) and Mike Bartlett's *King Charles III* (transferred to West End and Broadway and adapted for BBC television); Rebecca Frecknall's Olivier Award-winning production of Tennessee Williams' *Summer and Smoke* (transferred to West End); Robert Icke's productions of *Hamlet* and *Oresteia* (both of which transferred to New York) and *Mary Stuart* (West End and UK tour); and Lyndsey Turner's Olivier Award-winning production of Lucy Kirkwood's *Chimerica*.

www.nickhernbooks.co.uk

facebook.com/nickhernbooks

twitter.com/nickhernbooks